```
649                        12957
ARN      Arnstein, Helene S.  895
              The roots of love
```

DATE DUE

```
649.              12957
     Arnstein, Helene
 The roots of love.
                          8.95
JUL 28                   295
```

The ROOTS of LOVE

Previous books by Helene S. Arnstein:

WHAT TO TELL YOUR CHILD
About Birth, Illness, Death, Divorce
and Other Family Crises

YOUR GROWING CHILD AND SEX

**GETTING ALONG WITH YOUR
GROWN-UP CHILDREN**

BILLY AND OUR NEW BABY

**WHAT EVERY WOMAN NEEDS TO KNOW
ABOUT ABORTION**

Helene S. Arnstein

The ROOTS of LOVE

Helping Your Child Learn to Love in the First Three Years of Life

THE BOBBS-MERRILL COMPANY, INC.
INDIANAPOLIS/NEW YORK

Imperial Public Library
Imperial, Texas

Grateful acknowledgement is made to *The New York Times Magazine* for permission to reprint material from "That Old-Time Rock" by Helene S. Arnstein, © 1968 The New York Times, and to *Parents' Magazine*, New York, for permission to reprint in modified form portions of the article "How Babies Learn to Wait" by Helene S. Arnstein, © 1970 Parents' Magazine, New York.

Copyright © 1975 by Helene S. Arnstein

All rights reserved, including the right of
reproduction in whole or in part in any form
Published by the Bobbs-Merrill Company, Inc.
Indianapolis/New York

ISBN 0-672-51845-7
Library of Congress catalog card number 74-17674

Designed by Sheila Lynch
Manufactured in the United States of America

Second Printing

Contents

Preface   xiii

PROLOGUE

CHAPTER ONE

The Power of Love in Early Life   3
    Early Love—the Model for Later Love   4
    Anger, Hate, and Aggression   4
    Aggression Is Also Positive   5
    Children Starved for Love   8
    Is It All Up to Mother—and Father?   10
    Mother Today   11
    Does Society Mold the Individual or Vice Versa?   14

THE PARENTS

CHAPTER TWO

And Baby Makes Three   19
    Marriage Is Never the Same Again   20
    The New Mother and Her Mother   22
    Grandparents   25
    The New Importance of Father in the Early Years   26
    The "Baby Blues"   31
    Love at First Sight?   32
    Mother and Baby—Mix or Match?   33

Contents

THE BABY UNDER SIX MONTHS OF AGE
CHAPTER THREE

Love Needs of the Infant 37
   The Newborn 37
   The "Me" and "Thee" 38
   Substitutes for Mother in the Earliest Months 42
   Cueing In to Your Baby—the Beginnings of Communication 43
   Feeding and Love: Baby Doth Not Live by Milk Alone 45
   Feedings and Attitudes Toward Life 48
   The Meanings of the Baby's Cries 51
      Colicky Babies 54
   The Baby's Smile 54

CHAPTER FOUR

Soothing, Stimulating, and Spoiling 58
   Soothing 59
      The Cradle 59
      The Rocking Chair 61
      More Motion 62
      Touch 63
      Sucking 66
      Thumbs 67
      Pacifier 68
      Sound 68
   Stimulating 70
   Spoiling 72

THE BABY FROM SIX MONTHS TO A YEAR
CHAPTER FIVE

The Birth of Love 79
   Reactions to Strangers 81
   Reactions to Separation 83
   Brief Separations 85
      Peek-a-Boo 85
      Taking Leave of a Crying Baby 86

Contents

The Working Mother   88
Happiness Is a Cuddly Something   91
Emotional Aspects of Weaning   92
   Weaning from the Breast   92
   Weaning from the Bottle   94
Separating from Mother—on His Own   95

THE ONE- TO TWO-YEAR-OLD
                    CHAPTER SIX

The Toddler's Love Affair with the World   101
   The Young Explorer   101
   Trials and Tribulations of Mother and Toddler   105
   "No!"   107
   Special Parental Hangups   109
   Is This Being "Permissive"?   112
   "How Am I Doing?" or, Building Up Self-Esteem   114
   Separation Fears Again—New Sleep Problems   117

THE TWO- TO THREE-YEAR-OLD
                    CHAPTER SEVEN

Learning Impulse Control through Love   125
   Control of Bowel and Bladder   125
      Early Versus Later Training   126
      Newer Attitudes   127
      Wanting to Please Mother   129
   Control of Anger   131
      Fear of Loss of Love   132
      Using Love as a Weapon   136
      Handling the Anger and Tantrums   137
   Control Through Spanking?   139
      Might Is Right   140
      The Development of Conscience and Spanking   141
      Common Misconceptions About Spanking   141
   Learning to Cope with Jealousy and Rivalry   143
      Understanding How the Child Feels   144
      Preparing the Child   145

Contents

Helping the Child Accept His Feelings, yet Curb His Actions 146
Later Reactions to Brother or Sister 148

INFANCY TO THREE YEARS OF AGE

CHAPTER EIGHT

Longer Separations from Parents: Threats to Love 153
Nursery School and Separation 154
Easing the Child into His New Life 154
When the Child Hesitates 157
Mother's Feelings 159
The Working Mother and Day Care 160
Day Care for the Under-Threes, and Overall Hints 162
When Parents Take Vacations 163
Should We or Should We Not Go? 163
Planning for the Child 165
Possible Reactions Upon Your Return 166
When Parents Divorce 168
The Infant 169
The Child from Two to Three—and Over 171
Guilts and Fears 172

CHAPTER NINE

Healthy Sex Attitudes, Identity, and Development 175
How Sex Attitudes Develop 176
Genital Self-Discovery: the Boy 176
Genital Self-Discovery: the Girl 177
Masturbation 178
Discovery of Sex Differences: the Boy 179
Discovery of Sex Differences: the Girl 182
Birth Fantasies of Young Children 184
Sex Identity and Sex Roles 186
Do Little Boys and Girls Play with the Same Toys? 188
How Children Tell the Difference Between Adult Males and Females 191
Sex Role Identity 191

Contents

Healthy Sex Development   193
   The Boy and His Parents   195
   The Girl and Her Parents   197
   Other Suggestions for Helping the Child   199

EPILOGUE

CHAPTER TEN

Where Do We Go from Here?   203

Bibliography   209
Index   223

Preface

This is a book about feelings—the feelings of babies, of very young children, and of their parents. It is not a text on child development. Although I have followed some of the patterns of growth in a chronological sequence, I have not dealt with developmental stages as such. Rather, I have concentrated on feelings that are part of these stages, how they start and how they develop. I firmly believe that however useful general guides may be—and I do suggest some guides here and there—ultimately, each parent and each set of parents must find their unique way of communicating with their unique child. Every small being has his own needs, and all small beings have some needs in common. I hope to alert parents to some of these basic needs and to show how essential it is that they be met for the well-being and happiness of *all* family members.

I hope this book will not be labeled "sexist" because of the use of the generic "he" in referring to the child of either sex. Any other approach—and I have tried several—makes for clumsy or impersonal sentences.

My debt is great to the many who have made this book possible. I have listed only some of the works that have either directly or indirectly guided my thinking. Since certain of these books and papers have influenced several chapters, I have grouped them all in a single bibliography.

I wish to thank the many young mothers who shared their feelings and experiences with me. I am also most grateful to Betsey Fox Genovese, whose sensitive reading of the manuscript contributed another perspective to my thinking.

Preface

My deepest gratitude goes to Aline B. Auerbach, Consultant in Mental Health and Parent Education; Dr. Sylvia Brody, Adjunct Professor of Psychology, Graduate Center of the City University of New York; and Dr. Peter Neubauer, Director of the Child Development Center in New York City and Clinical Professor of Psychiatry, Downstate Medical Center, New York—all of whom carefully read earlier drafts of each chapter, giving me invaluable critical comments and suggestions.

To my editor at Bobbs-Merrill, Betty Kelly—herself a mother of two very young children—goes much appreciation, not only for her editorial expertise, but even more for believing in this book from the very start.

My husband Bill, as always, gave unsparingly of his time to read and evaluate each chapter. He patiently encouraged my efforts and, most of all, lived through the writing of it with me! My greatest debt and most loving gratitude are reserved for my two grown children and three very young grandchildren, who have been my best teachers; time and time again their selves and lives confirm the philosophy and beliefs expressed in this book.

PROLOGUE

CHAPTER ONE

The Power of Love in Early Life

Each newborn infant carries within himself life's greatest promise: a new hope for the world. For each tiny baby has the potential to love and be loved, to value himself yet care for others, to develop his unique abilities and talents and one day become a human being who can help change the world—for the better.

This outcome, of course, will depend upon a multitude of factors and many years of living and growing. But many of those who work in the field of mental health now believe that the baby's experiences of loving care during his* first three years of life are the most important and decisive for his future ability to love, to enjoy his work, and to get along with himself and others.

Everyone is born with the capacity to love, to form human attachments. In some this capacity is nourished from the moment of birth. In others it is underfed—or starved. The power of love is so strong in these earliest years that it can make sick babies well, as its lack can make well babies sick. This love has such a positive force that it can lessen and shorten the child's inevitable moments of frustration, anger, and hate. And it can modify these feelings, gradually channeling them into actions that are constructive, and later on in life toward great achievements.

* Note again: "He" or "she" means he or she or his or hers throughout the book unless otherwise specified.

EARLY LOVE— THE MODEL FOR LATER LOVE

It is a generally accepted fact that the reciprocal bonds and attachments formed in the very first years between the infant and his caregivers become models for his loves and relationships in adulthood. Good early "mothering" makes a man or woman capable of deep and enduring relationships. Our enjoyment in caressing and being caressed, in holding and being held, our enjoyment in the sensuous delights of our own and each other's bodies, all have their roots in these earliest love experiences.

The quality of the love life of every adult is patterned to a great degree upon the quality of love he received from the person who meant "Mother" to him, from infancy on through his third year. Memory traces of this first love remain deep in the core of our psychic life, long after they are consciously "forgotten." As Dr. Willie Hoffer, a psychoanalyst, trained in Vienna, once wrote, "the child needs his mother's love in order to be able to love himself, in order to do without her love; then he should be able to love another person as he was loved by his mother."

ANGER, HATE, AND AGGRESSION

But all is not sweetness and light. Even an infant, healthy and happy, has his dark moments. He feels cold, hungry, lonely, has gas pains, and is occasionally overtired. He frequently responds to his discomforts by lashing out with his arms and legs, using his lungs too as he tells the world how he feels. This is what we might call rage and aggression in an adult.

Anger and aggression—in an infant? Surely these impulses do not exist as we know them, but they exist, in miniature. Anyone who has ever seen a distressed infant turn beet-red as he screams and flails his limbs wildly can testify to his rage. His anger, which at first is not directed at anyone in particular, is his response to tensions and pain which he is helpless to remedy, or which no one else is successfully remedying at the moment. His uncomfortable feelings then are expressed actively—some call it assertively

—with the howls that are his way of saying, "Don't just *stand* there, *do* something!"

You can testify that these angry feelings and aggressive actions exist if you have ever witnessed a frustrated toddler grab a hunk of his playmate's hair and tug with all his might. If you have watched a tot start to clobber the head of his smaller or bigger brother or sister with a toy shovel, or in a fury knock down another youngster's toy tower, or kick his mother's shins in a temper, then you have witnessed the acting out of anger and hate—fierce, although short-lived.

All these emotions—anger, hate, resentment, guilt, fear, even jealousy—come in one package, although they are often slightly jumbled up. It is frequently hard to tell them apart. As adults, we are angry at, and hate, anyone we fear. We are angry and hate when we are put down; made to feel unimportant or powerless. We are angry and hate anyone who frustrates us and blocks our efforts. And when we are jealous and fear someone is trying to steal the affections of one we love—fearing besides that we may lose that love—we are angry and hate, and sometimes feel guilt besides.

Very young children can experience these often overwhelming emotions just as do adults. But many of us—unfortunately, not all—learned as we grew up how to deal with our feelings. We learned that it is one thing to *feel* like doing in our parents, siblings, playmates, and later on our neighbor, boss, or mother-in-law, and it is quite another thing to *do* it; to act out that feeling.

AGGRESSION IS ALSO POSITIVE

Many people assume that aggression is always something to be dreaded; that it means violence, attack, and destruction. Actually, aggression is a life force and energy that can be constructive as well as destructive. This force—call it assertiveness, if you will—is what makes an infant take hold of life and makes him yell for his food. It is part of his survival kit and may also be a healthy signal for help.

The Roots of Love

Dr. Albert J. Solnit, Professor of Pediatrics and Psychiatry, and Director of the Child Study Center at Yale University, points out that critically ill, hospitalized babies between the ages of about five months and a year need one special caretaking person: a mother or mothering figure, a nurse to whom they can cling and onto whom they can aggressively discharge feelings of irritation and anger that come from their pain or discomfort. This human target, Dr. Solnit explains, is one who at the same time soothes and cuddles the baby and gives him the loving and stimulating attention that he needs in order to respond well to the medical treatment he receives. Dr. Solnit says that "recovery is often accompanied by irritable, disagreeable behavior." Aggressive behavior in this sense becomes a necessary reaching-out step toward recovery and health. (The absence of such behavior worries doctors.)

Aggression, then, is necessary for survival, for self-preservation. It helps people to grow and develop and experience. It helps us all to master life, succeed, build bridges, love, mate, and procreate. Used in the service of love and achievement, or for the protection of the self and of others, aggression is constructive. Aggression, of course, is destructive when used in the service of hate; to take things away from others, to attack others—or the self (as in self-punishment).

How, then, do children learn how to use their aggressive drives constructively?

Here is where the power of love enters in.

As the infant receives comforting when in distress, as he experiences pleasure and satisfaction at the hands, and in the anchoring arms, of his loving partners—his parents or loving substitutes—he looks forward to this consistent nurturing. The responsive faces and smiles of those who tenderly care for him make him feel *enjoyed*. He begins to perceive himself and the world around him as "good" and, in his rather unformed way, begins to feel that exquisite sensation of being loved. Because he has learned to count on people, he is able to wait a little for their responses to his needs, certain that those responses will come his way. And in trusting expectation, he manages to tolerate

The Power of Love in Early Life

"bite-sized" bits of frustration. And later, through the young child's desire to secure the happy feelings of affection and approval from his loved ones, he slowly learns how to behave in a way that will please them.

Once they have felt love, the dread of its loss motivates both adult and child to hold back many impulses, and toe the line.

But parents help the child in his first introductions to life. As they continue to encourage him to see himself and the people around him as good, he slowly builds up what will later become a reasonable self-love and self-esteem—essential ingredients for loving others. In trusting himself, he trusts others. It takes a lot, then, to make him feel put down or frustrated, and it takes a lot to make him feel violently jealous. His hates and angers are apt to be fleeting, and he is more likely to let that part of his aggressive drives—his assertiveness—go out to meet the challenges of life with some optimism.

None of this takes place overnight. Such developments come about only after years of parental support. However, everything has a beginning, and these attitudes take root in early infancy and childhood.

While as parents we can do a lot to lessen the occurrence and intensity of painful feelings in the very young, we cannot spare a child from all psychic pain. Being loved, and being able to love, cannot guarantee against some inner conflict, dissatisfactions, disappointments, or life's unforeseen tragedies. And love cannot guarantee a perfectly adjusted child or adult. There is no such person. Yet the kind and quality of loving you can give, and your ability to understand what the infant and child needs at various ages and stages, along with understanding your own responses and needs, can do more than you can even imagine to help him cope with hardships, both in childhood and in adulthood.

This kind of loving, the essence of which will be described throughout the book, may provide him with an emotional storage bank from which he can draw when the going is rough. It may help to develop in him a rich personality, a zest for life, an ability to postpone "instant" gratification of his needs, and give him the strength to wait for the rewards of his efforts. And it may help him to be constant and responsible in his love relationships.

CHILDREN STARVED FOR LOVE

How have we come to discover that these first years of nurturing are of such vital importance to the emotional growth and stability of the child—and, later, adult?

In the sciences of human relationships, psychiatry, child development, in all the behavioral sciences that are not "exact" sciences, it is difficult to "prove" anything. However, findings come from the clinic, from thousands of studies and records of unhappy or disturbed children and adults that give repeated evidence of the influences on later life of unsatisfactory love relationships and experiences in early life. Furthermore, there are a large number of ongoing studies and observations of quite "normal" children conducted over a period of years, some of them following children from infancy on to school age, that clearly illustrate the positive or negative effect of early emotional life. Numerous studies undertaken in the past twenty-five years or so have revealed the tragic results in the lives of children who have been deprived of love or attachment in the early years.

Long before these studies were begun, however, an ancient and poignant story came to be known to many workers in the field of child care development.

A Holy Roman emperor, Frederick II, who lived in the thirteenth century was eager to discover in what language orphaned children would first speak if no one talked to them beforehand. Would it be Hebrew, Greek, Latin, or Arabic? Or would it be the language of their natural mother? The emperor then brought together a group of these orphaned infants and told their foster mothers and nurses to suckle them, to keep them clean, but not to prattle or murmur to them, and certainly not to speak to them. Unfortunately, the emperor never did find out the answer to his questions, because the babies all died. "For," as a chronicler of those times, Salimbene, wrote, "they could not live without the petting and joyful faces and loving words of their foster mothers."

The Power of Love in Early Life

Although infants who are deprived of affection yet receive adequate physical care do not all die, studies centuries later, on institutionally reared children, brought out further shocking facts that almost revolutionized the care of homeless infants and children in this and other countries.

In the late 1940s, Dr. René Spitz, Anna Freud, Dorothy Burlingham, Dr. John Bowlby, and other distinguished international and American child psychiatrists, child psychoanalysts, and pediatricians studied children living in various kinds of institutions under varying circumstances and degrees of deprivation.

In one foundling home examined by Dr. Spitz which housed ninety-one infants, the children had been breast-fed by their mothers during their first three months of life, or by another mother if their own mother wasn't available. At the time the children were tested, they had the appearance and development of any normal children of that age. But after those first three months, the babies were separated from their mothers. One nurse had the job of caring for twelve babies. Consequently, the infants were properly fed and kept clean and given good medical care, but they received no personal handling or affection. They received no "petting," they saw no "joyful faces," and they heard no "loving words." As Dr. Spitz wrote, "They got approximately one-tenth of the normal [emotional] supplies provided in the usual mother-child relationship." They began to suffer from emotional starvation.

Deterioration set in rapidly. Within three months the babies became depressed and just lay passive and listless in their cribs. Without being played with, fondled, or responded to, without any stimulation, their facial expressions became empty, often imbecilic. By the end of their second year, their average intelligence showed a marked decline. In the intelligence tests they came out 45 percent of normal—at the idiot level. The babies were so far gone that they gave no response whatsoever to the face or figure of anyone who approached them. Dr. Spitz continued, "by that time, with a few exceptions, these children

The Roots of Love

[could] not sit, stand, walk, or talk." In a number of cases the children simply wasted away and died.

Through these discoveries, as mentioned previously, many institutions today (although not all, by a long shot) have vastly improved their methods of meeting the needs of infants and very young children. And doctors frequently prescribe "TLC" for sick babies in hospitals when their own mothers cannot be with them. When nurses see these letters on the chart they know these abbreviations are not for a drug, but simply for "Tender, Loving Care."

IS IT ALL UP TO MOTHER— AND FATHER?

All of the above may be heavy going, but it is not meant to spell the voice of doom. Your child has not been, nor will he be, deprived of love or else you would not be reading this book. Besides, none of what has been said means you need to hover over your baby every moment to give him "love." Likewise, you do not have to, nor could you, fill every single one of his needs and guarantee that he is never disappointed. No matter how hard one tries—as we will see later—this cannot be accomplished. Nor is it necessary or even desirable. The mere idea of such all-inclusive attention is totally unrealistic, since life with all of its other business must go on. And just a small amount of tension that is soon relieved motivates a child's growth.

Nor should the above mean that all is lost if a child hasn't had the very best emotional life in his first three years, due to illness, family troubles, or crises—all to be discussed later—granted that these first three years lay the cornerstone of mental health. As a child develops, he goes through various stages. (The German word for development is *entwicklung*, which means "unfolding," or "unwinding.") A child's development can be looked at in this way, for if he is surrounded by caring persons, he actually unfolds like a surprise ball, revealing new delights; his first smile, words, steps, and so on! Each rung in the ladder of his development successfully passed makes the next rung that much easier to reach. But, if there have been some breaks along the developmental lines for varied reasons, the lines can usually be repaired. Yet it is also true that the older the child beyond these three years, the more effort, patience, understanding, and love it takes to make the repairs. Often, skilled professional help is then needed.

Naturally, there are many influences besides parental love that also affect the child's emotional growth during his early years. We know there is an unknown factor: a child's biological inheritance, his inborn constitution and personality. Some children are more sensitive to life than others. Some children are more prone to anxiety; some have more aggressive, more assertive energy. Others are more passive. And then there are the circumstances of life. Where a mother faces poverty and discrimination, and perhaps single-handedly struggles for mere survival for herself and her young ones, it is quite possible that her anger, bitterness, fatigue, and despair can adversely affect her relationship with her children. Nevertheless, in some such homes, exceptionally strong love bonds and courage have held families together in spirit and dignity in spite of almost unbearable pressures. One cannot be too optimistic either about the emotional development of children who, at an early age, have witnessed violence, brutality, drug addiction, and sexual promiscuity, and whose homes are so disorganized that the child has no one central person with whom he can form strong ties. At the same time, even under such horrendous circumstances, there may be one caring relative whose love has fostered and strengthened that particular child's emotional life through these severe trials.

In general, however, this book is primarily addressed to families who have the no-more-than-usual problems of family living; the ups and downs, the financial worries, the disagreements, the crises—along with the satisfactions; in other words, the "average" family.

MOTHER TODAY

In certain groups today, the word "motherhood" has almost become a bad word, if not obsolete. It has turned into an

The Roots of Love

embarrassment for some mothers. They even feel apologetic if they *enjoy* their role of being a fairly full-time mother when their children are very young, while formerly they felt apologetic if they even entertained the idea of working part-time. The words "fairly full-time" are being used advisedly because the mother of a very young baby or young child who is supposed to be on call twenty-four hours a day certainly needs to get away from this job occasionally. True, motherhood in the past was oversentimentalized, eulogized, and sanctified. Many sins like "momism" have been perpetrated on innocent children under the guise of "motherly love" and "sacrifice" through which the children were smothered more than mothered. Often these mothers depended totally on their children to derive a sense of worth and achievement ("my children are my greatest pride"), with sorry results for all.

Today, women have choices. They can decide to have or not to have a baby or two (the average family in the United States at present has something like 1.9 children—a new low). And if they want children, they still have choices. They may opt to stay at home and be with their babies and young children, or they may opt to work full- or part-time, or take up community activities, or study or work at home while their babies are under two or three years of age. Such decisions need never be final. Today they are open-ended. Of course, a mother may have to work full-time because her career cannot wait for her, or she has no choice but to support or help to support her family. Still another mother may simply prefer a job outside of the home. Difficult adjustments lie ahead for all of these mothers who choose to or have to make a livelihood when their children are so very young. But with careful thought and planning, and with help from her husband, if she has one, a working mother may be able to make suitable arrangements so that her young child's emotional life will not suffer.

Although motherhood in the old-fashioned sense of the word may be "out," *mothering*—and *fathering* too—is "in." Both mother and father today are eager to know how to give their babies and young children the very best start. Many mothers are particu-

The Power of Love in Early Life

larly concerned about when, how, and for how long their babies and toddlers can tolerate being separated from them, and how their young will take to substitute care at the various stages of the early months and years. Much of this will be carefully spelled out in later chapters.

A woman who chooses to become a mother will find her role a tremendous source of fulfillment. But it is just one part of her total fulfillment. Being an *individual,* a *person,* a *wife* are all other parts of the sum total. Strangely enough, the more fulfilled and the happier a mother feels—no matter what she is "doing" or not doing outside the home—the more she can give freely of herself to her child. The pleasure she gets out of life is sure to rub off on her baby. He is quick to catch the "vibes" around him. At the same time, child rearing, as with all jobs, occupations, careers, or relationships, has its moments of ennui, drudgery, despair, irritation, worry, and sheer exhaustion. But there are also moments of great joy, fun, contentment, enrichment, satisfaction, and delight.

Some years ago the emphasis on child care was on "what to do and when." Then another ingredient was added: "how to." Now it is not so much the individual parental action that has import but rather the feelings and attitudes that accompany this action. (This goes for feeding, weaning, toilet-training, etc.) An even newer dimension has been included on the list: *relationships.* In this context, relationships means the way in which people in a family "relate" to each other, respect one another, feel and empathize with each other. It includes the particular feelings that are exchanged between parents, between parents and their children, between parents and their own parents—and the feelings that a husband and wife have about themselves.

Today's young parents are sharing child-rearing and home responsibilities to a degree that sometimes startles their elders. Family chores are no longer segregated along strictly defined male and female roles, i.e., "This is a man's job," or "That is woman's work." A new flexibility and ease have come about with "human liberation," as well as a more cooperative spirit of true partnership in family living. Everyone in the family is recognized

The Roots of Love

as having "rights," and that goes for Mother, Father, *and* Baby. A family that can pull together even when life becomes full of pressures and tribulations will be working not only toward solidarity, but toward the goals of mutual growth, respect, and love.

DOES SOCIETY MOLD THE INDIVIDUAL OR VICE VERSA?

Is it the individual who, acting with the cooperation of others, molds society, or is it the society, sick or healthy, that shapes the individual? This question, of course, is like asking the perennial riddle, "Which came first, the chicken or the egg?"

Many years ago when Margaret Mead was studying the sex roles and lives of some primitive peoples in New Guinea, she also traced the way in which one of these tribes, the gentle, cooperative Arapesh, raised their young, and the way in which another tribe, the fierce and cannibalistic Mundugumors, raised theirs—each with their own view of what was necessary to produce the kind of men and women their society needed.

Observing that the Arapesh had easygoing, warm, trusting, and cooperative personalities, Dr. Mead wrote in *Sex and Temperament*:

> It is true that in any simple and homogeneous society the children will as adults show the same general personality traits that their parents have shown before them. But this is not a matter of simple imitation. A more delicate and precise relationship obtains between the way in which the child is fed, put to sleep, disciplined, taught self-control, petted, punished, and encouraged, and the final adjustment. Furthermore, the way in which men and women treat their children is one of the most significant things about the adult personality of any people . . .

In this tribe the babies are held a great deal and suckled whenever they cry. A baby sleeps in close contact with his mother's body, "either hung in a thin net bag against her back, crooked in her arm or curled in her lap as she sits cooking and

The Power of Love in Early Life

plaiting, and the child has a continuous warm sensation of security." The fathers too are maternal and warm, and the baby is never left alone; the comforting human skin and voices of his parents and others are always there. Even other little boys and girls adore babies and are willing to cuddle and hold the baby for his mother when she is busy. The child soon learns to trust and love and depend on all those with whom he has contact. So certain that he will be well treated, the baby "follows happily the last member of the kind world who tickles its stomach, or scratches its always itching little back. Children wriggle about on the ground from one friendly adult to another, settling down beside anyone who pays definite attention to them." This kind of tender affection sets up the child's emotional pattern for his future, Dr. Mead observes. By the time the Arapesh children are seven or eight years of age, their personalities are firmly set. They have a trusting, confident attitude toward life, and have been discouraged from any display of hostile aggressiveness. In addition they now treat the property, the sleep, and the feelings of others with respect and consideration.

In contrast, the competitive and vengeful Mundugumors have a totally different value system. All men, even father and son or brothers, are hostile to one another in the extreme. Rivalry and distrust run high. In fact, all men are sworn enemies, and if they aren't fighting one another physically, they insult one another in anger, always feeling "wronged." A man is judged by his success alone, which includes the number of wives he can manage to collect.

The child is born into an angry, unloving world where the father has resented his unborn child from the moment of his wife's pregnancy. A baby is carried about in a stiff, uncomfortable basket suspended from his mother's forehead, with his arms almost pinioned to his sides. Since the basket is tightly woven, the baby can see nothing but a tiny bit of light. When he cries, the baby is not fed immediately, and when he *is* suckled, the mother stands holding the child firmly with one hand, completely restraining his movements. Mother and child derive no sensuous pleasure during the feeding process. Rather, the infant is rushed

The Roots of Love

through his feeding to such a point that he often starts to choke, since he has to swallow his food so fast. In turn, the mother is angered by the choking and shows her anger to the child. As one can well imagine, the weaning, although it takes place very late, is abrupt and accompanied by blows and nasty words.

When the children are ill or meet with accidents—not infrequent—the parents act with exasperation and become sulky and resentful. The children who *do* survive learn to be tough. The child's disciplining, with many restraints, is severe. And so it goes until adulthood, when the child becomes the type of adult just described. Girls fare just a bit better; they too can fight physically with their men, who, however, can subdue them by making them pregnant!

To return to contemporary life. Parenting, with the hopes of raising children to become loving, warm, and giving humans, can make this world a better one for all of us. Hate narrows as love expands, and this love can reach out in a wide circle that includes and is felt by many others. People gravitate to families who shed this warmth, friendliness, and openness.

Perhaps, as sensitive parents, we may be able to effect a tremendous change in our society through our offspring. Everyone complains bitterly about the ills of our times—the prevalence of crime and violence, the many who suffer from feelings of loneliness, isolation, and a sense of detachment and emptiness. In trying to seek surcease from years and years of accumulated pain starting in early childhood, some of these unhappy ones desperately "turn on" with drugs, join cults, enter into "instant therapies" that spring up overnight and cure little. (One writer calls these therapies "thrift shops of the psyche.")

Maybe we can make a new start and put our minds and hearts to the very things that can help to create a generation of magnificent human beings, who truly know and love themselves as well as others, who can use their aggressive energies creatively, for the betterment of life for all.

As we strengthen the very roots of life and love in each tiny baby, in each little child, perhaps we may come closer to realizing that dream.

THE PARENTS

 CHAPTER TWO

And Baby Makes Three

It is always easier to give out love, to care for another human being and anticipate his needs, when one's own earliest needs have been met. Parenting also comes easier to those who have had their own fill of nurturing. But parents need not have had a perfect childhood—which of us has?—to love their own children and give out love to them. Indeed, those who are *aware* of this lack often make conscious efforts to give their child more affection and emotional nurturance than they received. And the feedback may be sheer joy!

Although the giving-out to a helpless, totally dependent baby can be a deep and long-lasting satisfaction, no one can always be on the giving end of life. Every adult needs to be loved and even babied at times, especially when tired or ill. And these legitimate needs, often buried, may surface with particular force before and after the birth of a baby. Surprisingly, just the realization that such feelings are par for the course can often make their demands seem less pressing.

This exciting, very special little seven- or eight-pound bundle of responsibilities who has come into your lives is, like most blessings, a mixed one. Both a delight and a burden, the newly arrived can rock the marriage boat or steady its course. The outcome depends largely on how well the baby's mother and father can continue to sustain each other's needs for love and support—even as these needs change and as the marriage changes.

MARRIAGE IS NEVER THE SAME AGAIN

"The arrival of the first child transforms spouses into parents and turns a marriage into a family," says Dr. Theodore Lidz, Professor, Department of Psychiatry, Yale University School of Medicine. Dr. Lidz goes on to say, "The endless drama has curved around to face the beginning of life; but now the players are taking the parents' nurturant and supportive roles that they learned when they were ingénues playing the children's part; but the old lines do not quite fit, and constant improvisation is required."

Our role as parents is part of everything we've ever been, are, or hope to be. All kinds of thoughts and feelings from way back in our life histories are woven into parenthood. They appear at the oddest moments to enhance or disrupt the pattern. The marriage fabric itself has to stretch in love and time and attention to accommodate the newcomer. As one recent mother put it, "It's no longer just 'me for you and you for me,' as the song goes. And it sure is hard getting used to a third party cutting in."

The carefree, easy days are over. You are tied down. You may begin to miss the stimulus of your set-aside career, or the buzzing of your office life, or all the absorbing activities in which you were once engaged. No longer free to take a trip, or go out to a restaurant, to a movie, or to the discothèque, there are always arrangements to consider for Baby. "Will the distance or the weather affect him?" "Where would we put the porta-crib?" "Suppose the baby starts crying?" "Could we safely leave him with a sitter?"

Many weary nights of broken sleep are ahead. And there may be nights when you suddenly hear Baby's insistent cries while you are making love. Strangely enough, all of these, and other inroads on young parents' lives, all of these interruptions of the former serenity of marriage now altering their life style, can also become a challenge in working out ways of meeting these

And Baby Makes Three

problems. Coming to grips with the new demands that descend upon them often brings a couple closer together than ever before.

But there is a period of adjustment.

The need to share love and life with a third party often makes some of us race back twenty-five or thirty years or so in time—unconsciously, of course—to those days when we were tiny children and were the exclusive love (or so we fantasied) of our mother. Then, perhaps we slowly discovered that Mother was not ours alone, or a new baby arrived on the scene to spoil things for us. The child in us, which is never fully outgrown, may still feel faint stirrings of that jealousy emerging now in relation to our own newborn.

Take as an example a new father's feelings when his wife becomes so totally engrossed in her baby that he feels stranded, somewhere out in left field. These feelings of being put upon can also be triggered during pregnancy when a father-to-be is sometimes asked to give *more* emotionally to his wife at a time when she—absorbed with what is taking place within her body—gives *less* to him!

One husband who felt displaced by his baby stated bitterly, "Lucy never thinks of me any more. When I used to come home from work she'd be mixing martinis. Now she's mixing formulas!" This man's perception of the situation that made him feel his baby was a rival for his wife's affections was also colored in part by his childhood experience, when he had felt that his newborn brother had usurped his place with his mother.

One mother of a six-week-old girl felt her husband was lavishing all of his affections on the baby. The first words he uttered as he came in through the door each evening were, "How's Nancy?" and, ignoring her, would rush over to pick up the infant. This young mother in turn was craving a little fathering for herself and wanted to hear her husband ask, "How was *your* day, darling?" and then take her in his arms.

While a husband and wife will sometimes seem father and mother as well as lover and friend to each other, the real marital relationship can become somewhat blurred when a husband sees his wife *exclusively* as a mother figure, or when a wife sees her husband *only* as a father image. The husband may want his wife to give him all the unconditional love he received—or did not receive—from his mother. His wife may want to lean upon him as she always leaned upon her father. Or, she may fear and expect the same cool indifference she experienced with her father, as a child, and be hurt by every seeming slight from her husband.

Dr. Lidz indicates, "Even mature persons seek something of a parent in a spouse." It is all a matter of degree naturally. "The capacity of a spouse to be protectively and affectionately parental," Dr. Lidz adds, "and conversely to be able to permit the other to provide solace can be particularly important during times of stress. . . ." At such times the spouse who is upset can feel his troubles slowly disappear just through receiving "tangible evidence of being wanted and loved."

We experience mixed feelings about nearly everything in life and probably about everyone too. We love, yet we also are angry at times with the one we love. And the feelings that go with being a parent are no exception.

Somehow, any mother and father are apt to find parenthood smoother sailing if she and he are able to share their misgivings and express their doubts, fears, and longings. Our ability to communicate with one another, quietly, openly, without anger and resentment—which accumulates steam through hostile silence—can help us to expand in self-awareness and awareness of the other. This openness is also apt to lead to a greater awareness of the baby's needs, and to more enjoyment in sharing the delights he has to offer.

The sharing of new pleasures, hardships, tasks, hopes, and dreams via the baby can bring about a more profound sense of personal identity, growth, and fulfillment.

Marriage may never be the same again. But it may well be better.

THE NEW MOTHER AND HER MOTHER

A woman's sense of self-esteem and maturity goes up a peg when

And Baby Makes Three

she becomes a mother. Having moved into the same league as her own mother, she feels more truly her equal. A new and stronger bond begins to be forged between the two generations—a bond that soon includes the third.

Your accomplishment in giving birth to a baby not only provides *you* with joy, but is also in a way a gift to your husband, his parents, and your parents—especially your mother. The rejoicing of all the parents in the baby is deeply satisfying to you too.

Many new mothers, even during pregnancy, are drawn closer to their own mothers. (This is shown by the custom in many parts of the world of having mothers on hand at the time of childbirth.) Some daughters seek a reconciliation with their mothers after those years of not so long ago when adolescent and postadolescent needs for separation, independence, and the establishment of identity got in the way of closeness. Now, with the realization of a new identity as a parent, a new mother may find a greater readiness to ask her mother for help, as one adult to another. That is, as long as she feels she has outgrown her need to "prove" herself to her mother; in this particular situation, that *she* is an adequate parent. (Strong attempts to show one can get along without help often indicate a continued need to establish one's independence.)

Rich rewards are likely to be forthcoming in the new relationship with your mother. How gratifying to hear her say admiringly, "Susie stretches and yawns and puckers her mouth just as you did!" or the reassurances, "I was worried, too, when you used to fall asleep during your feedings. But you survived!"

If you were lucky enough to have had warm mothering, you may "remember" unconsciously those long-forgotten experiences of your preverbal days, and now, somehow, you just seem to know how to hold your baby in the curve of your arm, how to caress him and murmur to him. (No doubt, if you did some baby-sitting when you were a teen-ager, or if you had younger brothers or sisters, you may have had firsthand practical experience as well to help you along in those first uncertain days and weeks.) The very fact that you can mother your child so easily despite those shaky moments is a great compliment to this mother of yours. Whatever "mistakes" she made in your upbringing—which you will be anxious to avoid—her real feelings of love must have come through to you.

Yet often mothers find that some memories of angry moments, disappointments, or resentments connected with their own mothers are also reawakened at this time. They are determined to do better with *their* child-rearing tactics. "Baby's going to get everything I missed!"

Most likely you are going to do much better—in some respects. With it all, no parents are perfect or ideal—just as there is no ideal marriage, husband, or child. While one's mother and father may have made some errors with their children, a new mother and father are quite likely, without knowing it, to make some new mistakes all their own!

Often, as a mother begins to go through the experiences of mothering, she may discover a new compassion for her own mother. She may come to see that, in other days, mothers were not always as knowledgeable about mother-infant and mother-child relationships as are today's young mothers (and many did not have helping husbands). They did their own thing in the styles of those days, and the "how-to" styles of child-rearing have changed dramatically since then. In addition, there might have been some unavoidable happenings in the lives of families that had a strong effect on each member of the family: illness, serious difficulties between parents, divorce, death, etc. One mother told her mother, "I just marvel now over how you managed to take care of me when I was two during that terrible year of Dad's near-fatal auto accident."

Occasionally, however, relationships between mother and daughter remain strained and bitter. It can be that the older woman herself had serious emotional difficulties with *her* parents —some of which may have adversely affected her emotional relationship with her own daughter during the girl's growing years. And now these old resentments persist within the grown daughter, interfering with the present mother-daughter relationship. Insight perhaps, and some degree of objectivity, if possible, can help a daughter look at things as they are today, with a newer perspective, which may improve the situation. But if the wounds remain unhealed and still continue to fester in the younger woman's psyche, she may be helped to establish a more workable relationship with her mother by seeking the counsel of a skilled professional. With the lessening of some of her inner conflicts, the young mother may even learn to enjoy her mother in a new way.

GRANDPARENTS

Grandparents, long neglected, are being rediscovered today. The need for them is increasing in our impersonal world, even if they live some distance away. The strong need for human contact and connections, for kinship, for an extended circle of meaningful people in a child's life is greater today than ever before. The "nuclear family"—mother, father, and child (or children)—*seems* to have gone bankrupt! Small families find it a constant struggle to go it alone. These added loving attachments to grandparents, nourished in early childhood, are good insurance against the feelings of emptiness and loneliness that come to many in adult life. Children, even those under three years of age, need these extra adults to love and to trust. They are happy to know there are others outside of their main love objects, Mother and Father, who care for them. At the same time, the children are able to expand their own growing capacities to love and share affection. Visiting grandparents who come from far away often see their grandchildren around the clock and not just for a few hours at a time. Their grandchildren can also develop strong and lasting emotional ties with them through the intensity of these occasional but tightly packed visits.

On a more practical level, if you can call on the help of any of the grandparents in those early weeks, it may give you a chance to get out of the house to enjoy an evening with your husband, feeling especially secure that your baby is being well looked after. Should your mother or mother-in-law remind you of a drill sergeant as she tries to take over too much, remember her

The Roots of Love

dominion cannot last too long. As soon as you are able to take full hold of the reins in your household once again, you can politely but firmly point out that it is *your* turn now to mother, and you would love her help if she is willing to do the helping *your* way.

The husband and wife who feel secure in their own ability to parent are not likely to be too much bothered by the slightly different, or even quite different, child-rearing ways of a *loving* grandmother. After all, it is their own constant and consistent care that will be felt by the baby, rather than the relatively brief contact he has with Grandma.

Remember, too, you can brag and rave and marvel to your mother or mother-in-law over Baby's outstanding charms and ways without being considered a bore—as you surely would be to your friends! There comes a day also when your baby may know his grandparents so well that he will not mind one bit to have them look after him while you and your husband take off for a few days of a much-needed rest or change of scene.

THE NEW IMPORTANCE OF FATHER IN THE EARLY YEARS

Adlai Stevenson once said that many fathers have children but very few children have fathers. The late Ambassador's remark certainly described fathers of very young children—until quite recently. For generations, Father was considered a second-class citizen as far as his paternal role in his children's earliest years. That patriarchal, slightly distant, yet austere figure of the Victorian era protected and supported his family, disciplined the children, and passed on to them the life goals, values, and aspirations he lived by and cherished. As years went by, the father image continued pretty much along the traditional breadwinner and disciplinarian lines. Mother reinforced the threatening aspect of his image by shouting, "Wait till your father comes home! *He'll* have something to say about this!"; or, "He'll *give* it to you!"

In some families, children also may have had a warm and

And Baby Makes Three

personal relationship with their fathers, but often this relationship developed only after the little ones had emerged from the nursery years. One 49-year-old grandfather remarked, "My first memories of my father were the times when he asked me to show him my hands before we sat down to eat." Unfortunately, many a father may have secretly wanted to cuddle and nurture his baby but was afraid to because it wasn't customary or fashionable. It was considered "unmanly" behavior.

Times changed, and in many homes Father seemed to fade out of the family picture. He could be found at the office, quite often working late, or he could be found on the golf course or out fishing. And when at home, he could be found behind a newspaper. Child-rearing was left largely up to "Mom," who, without an active participating male partner (a father who may have been there, but not "there" emotionally), often developed a too-exclusive and intense relationship with her children—particularly with her male child.

More recently, however, Father has come out of the woodwork. He is right there, pitching in with Mother from the very start. Researchers in family life have begun to emphasize the significance of Father for the emotional well-being of each member of the family. His active role in child-rearing is considered necessary, not as an assistant mother, but as a father who has a special and specific role to play in the psychological and social development of his child.

In many sections of the country today men are being encouraged to take part in prenatal classes with their wives. Many give their wives support while they are in labor, rather than stride restlessly and aimlessly about in the hospital corridor, as in the past. Some fathers are even present during the actual delivery, profoundly moved by this experience. Sharing in these different but intimate ways builds up a father's feelings of being part of it all from the very beginnings of life.

A number of reasons have been offered for this turnabout in attitudes. No doubt the Women's Liberation movement has had something to do with it, yet these changes were becoming evident sometime before the movement got launched. "Hired help," as

The Roots of Love

they were called in some families, and "servants" in others, had become scarce. The young couple no longer had relatives living in the same home or close by to help in relieving the mother of the constant demands of her young. Many fathers noticed the emotional strains and drains on their wives, who tried to be everything to everybody. And so, numbers of husbands began to help further in the details of parenting, which became a "we" experience. Countless young couples getting a higher education wanted to have babies while they were both still young. This meant an increased number of young on-campus parents, taking turns in the caretaking of the baby while the other studied, attended classes, or worked part-time. And today, quite a few young fathers work at home while their wives continue their professional training or take jobs.

Perhaps more important from a psychological point of view, as our society has become more and more depersonalized, many men have found a greater need to derive emotional sustenance and gratification from their families. Edwin Nichols, a psychologist with the National Institute of Mental Health, suggests also that there has been a reaction of a generation of young men who themselves felt "abandoned" by their own fathers who had been away too often on business trips, or at war.

What then, is a "good" father? What is "fatherly"?

"Fatherliness," says Dr. Therese Benedek, psychiatrist and Senior Staff member of the Chicago Institute of Psychoanalysis, "is an instinctively rooted character trend which enables the father to act toward his child or all children with immediate empathic responsiveness."

Empathy—the ability to feel or understand what another person feels—first develops through the baby's earliest source of security, his mother. Men, born and cared for by their mothers, first identify with her and "see" the world, so to speak, through her eyes. Soon thereafter, in normal development, the boy begins to identify with his father, and feels himself a male. But part of him will always retain some of the qualities he took on from his mother—the so-called "feminine" part of himself—which is quite normal.

And Baby Makes Three

Dr. Benedek goes on to say, "A tender, loving father reinforces the male's acceptance of his own tender feelings; a rigid, strict and punitive father activates in the boy those defensive qualities, compels him to repress his tenderness, and thus inhibits the development of his fatherliness."

Similar to a mother's relationship with her own mother, when a man becomes the father of a son or daughter, he is no longer just a son, in competition with his "old man" and defensive, but rather he becomes his father's equal in status. The best preparation a young father can have for his new role is through the relationship he had with his own father or father figure when he was very young. In Wordsworth's famous words, "The child is father of the man."

During his wife's pregnancy, sometimes happy and maybe not-so-happy memories of his own childhood are stirred up, and a man may wonder whether he will be an adequate parent.

Memories such as these are described by Dr. Arthur Colman and his wife, Libby Lee Colman, M.A., in their book, *Pregnancy: The Psychological Experience*:

> The father-to-be may be flooded by forgotten images—playing ball, being tossed into the air, learning how to do household repairs with his father at his side, seeing his father hold him in the mirror and wondering who was who, feeling the living line between grandfather, father and son, and discovering immortality in a family name or nose. Then there are the disturbing residues; loneliness at being ignored by the provider, looking for male contact in a woman-dominated home and school, the fear of being hit by a raging, angry giant, or watching, helpless to intervene, as an argument between parents threatens to tear apart the foundations of his universe.

There are times when a young father may worry whether his son—if he has a son—will be angry with him just as he was angry with *his* father, or that he'll act out in anger toward the child as his father acted toward him.

One way through which an expectant or new father can be helped to resolve some of these conflicts with his own male parent and keep them from interfering in his relations with his new baby is to try to see his infant as an individual, separate in his makeup and body from his parents. As the young father begins to take a more rational view of the real situation, he may see before him a tiny infant who is ready to start from scratch to develop a very happy, unique, and loving bond with him.

There are many fathers who still take a rather dim view of diapering and feeding the baby, and who enjoy the child more after he has begun to talk and walk. In the meantime, a father can do many other things in the home to help a young mother juggle all the claims upon her time and emotions. Besides, he helps to recharge her emotional batteries when they are running low just by showing his love for her and the baby.

Yet the father who does take an active part from the earliest days of his baby's life may find some surprising rewards in the infant's response. While Father's arms may not be as soft and his chest not so well padded as Mother's, his secure and loving holding is happily felt by the baby. The infant begins to react to these paternal ministrations even during his first months of life. Soon thereafter, the baby begins to recognize his father's footsteps and reaches out to him with a smile and with his arms.

Studies have shown that in some families the child may become even more attached to his father, whom he sees little of but who freely responds to him when he comes home, than to a mother who takes care of the baby all day long but who may rarely approach him playfully and joyfully. And from London come some similar findings, as Dorothy Burlingham reports from the Hampstead Child-Therapy Clinic: "In all those instances where the special care of the children weighs heavily on the wife and interferes with her more lighthearted responses, the husband, less burdened, may be more ready to enter with a purely pleasurable father-infant relationship." The observations also indicated that fathers often were known to handle their infants very carefully and gently in the beginning for fear of hurting them, and some fathers would hear the baby's cry at night even before the mother!

The easing up of ancient notions of what is manly—and

tenderness is very manly—gives a father full rein to express his own nurturing urges. The gradual breaking down of society's outdated standards of "maleness" gives a young father one more dimension to his enjoyment of life.

Fathering, at last, has come into its own.

THE "BABY BLUES"

> Just Molly and me, and Baby makes three.
> We're happy in our blue heaven.

So go the lovely words of an old song popular in the twenties. And how unrealistic! An isolated "blue heaven" is the last thing today's young parents want or need when their baby is born. Rather, many young families are seeking ways of life in which they can be surrounded by warm friends and neighbors and other young parents if their own parents and relatives are not available. Anyone is fortunate who can call upon sisters, brothers, aunts, uncles, cousins—and mother and mother-in-law, as mentioned earlier. Whatever practical help and emotional support these others can offer in the early weeks after the baby's birth is manna from heaven. Furthermore, as the baby's orbit widens, he will be receiving extra love bonuses.

That blue heaven may really be blue at times. There are those days when many a young mother gets the temporary "baby blues," also called "maternity blues." These heavy feelings can descend upon a new mother any time during the first few weeks after the baby's birth.

There are various reasons for these moods. Quite a few medical authorities speak of the temporary hormonal changes that occur as the body becomes readjusted to its prepregnant state. Others point out that if heavy drugs are administered during childbirth, mothers may still have a hangover. Then there is the tired aftermath of the exertions of labor. Or, hearing the poignant cries of the baby makes many young mothers feel anxious and helpless. Still others claim that the new mother may experience a feeling of emptiness—having parted with something that was so very close to her for so long. And it often takes a while to form a new relationship with the baby that is now outside her body. Beyond this are some realities that can make anyone feel blue.

Quickly, so it seems, after a round of congratulations, flowers, cards, baby presents, and enthusing people visiting you and the baby, you are sent home from the hospital and thrown into a round of diaper-changing, formula or breast-feedings (the latter not always successful in the beginning), and exhausting nights of interrupted sleep. From a passive state in pregnancy, when you were turned in on yourself, you are forced to be active now—and maybe you don't feel quite up to it yet. At these moments many a mother has wondered, "Am I really ready to be a mother?" "Am I able to cope with it all?" It may be helpful to bear in mind that no one is every really "ready" to become a mother, to get married, or even to take on a difficult job. One can only learn by doing. Should such depressive feelings persist, however, it is important to let the doctor or the clinic know about them. Sometimes medications and/or professional counseling are needed.

LOVE AT FIRST SIGHT?

It is true. Many mothers do fall in love with their baby at first sight. They think he is the most beautiful and perfect baby that was ever born. And he may—or may not—be! Others, who do not experience instant motherhood, wonder, where is that surge of maternal love I'm supposed to feel? Maybe I'm not cut out to be a mother. Or they look at their baby and are somewhat disappointed that here is a girl instead of a boy, or vice versa. (For most parents sex preference soon disappears, and fortunately so, because a boy's or girl's sense of his or her sex identity is established primarily by being loved *as* a boy or girl. But more about this later.) Mothers sometimes lament, "Junior has Uncle Willy's receding chin and Father's long nose instead of my nose and Jack's chin!" And certainly this infant, often wrinkly or blotchy skinned, bald or hirsute, with a head that may seem elongated and features that look sat upon, is far removed from the baby you dreamed of or whose pictures you saw in the magazine ads. And it takes some convincing to believe that soon the baby's appearance *will* change and that he'll really take shape. Don't forget: those ad babies are usually six weeks to six months old.

Truly now, how many people *do* fall in love at first sight? Don't most of us need time to get acquainted with any new person in our lives? Aren't we eager to know more about his personality—how we "fit," how we respond to each other? Or, maybe this time it is an opposite-attracts relationship. By and large, a relationship begins to form gradually, through familiarity, and through the sharing of experiences—all of which takes time. And then those warm and loving feelings can develop.

Mother love doesn't always burst forth in full bloom. It is more apt to grow, step by step, even slowly sometimes. Some mothers feel maternal love when they are still pregnant and feel the baby's first kick or signs of life. Some experience tender feelings after they have fed their baby a few times. Others find themselves hooked after they have given their baby his first bath, or at that miraculous moment when he first smiles at them. Then there are mothers who confess, "You know, I got my first big charge out of Sally when she spoke her first real words."

Maternal feelings cannot be forced—nor should they be. They usually arrive in their own good time.

MOTHER AND BABY— MIX OR MATCH?

Perhaps you are a quiet, calm, even-tempered individual, and discover you are now the mother of a lusty, active baby who when he cries yells bloody murder. Or you may be a very lively, vigorous woman yourself and find your baby is docile, slow-moving, and takes forever with his feedings. Your baby may be very cuddly from the start—or maybe it will take him a long time to enjoy the cuddling you are so eager to give him.

Temperaments vary. Each child differs in his reactions and

The Roots of Love

responses, in his rate of growth and development, in the amount of sleep he requires and when, in how physically active he is, and in the amount of food he needs and will take. Once more it must be said that two people need *time* in order to adapt to each other and to their individual ways and needs. And, without their even knowing it, in any human relationship, people affect each other and can even change each other to a degree. A nervous, high-strung baby may become calmer, quieter, through a mother who ministers to him gently and securely.

No one can order a mother to "relax and enjoy your baby!" Yet these words do have some meaning. As a mother catches on to her baby's unique ways, she somehow does relax more and is therefore more able to enjoy him. The more she has confidence in herself as a person and as a mother (along with the ups and downs) the freer she will be to see and hear what the baby is trying to "tell" her by his cries and his motions. This does not mean that, for example, if your baby happens to cry a lot or will not finish his feedings you are not a "good" mother.

As you begin to find out more about your individual baby, partially through learning more about the reactions of other babies at different stages of development, and partially through trial and error on your part, you will eventually find ways of handling him that suit both of you—at least most of the time!

THE BABY
UNDER SIX MONTHS

CHAPTER THREE

Love Needs of the Infant

THE NEWBORN

After months of lying closely embraced by the warmth and darkness of his mother's womb, where he was lulled by her rhythmic breathing, by the regular sounds of her heartbeats and the gentle undulations and rocking motions of her walking, the infant is suddenly catapulted out of his comfortable nest and rudely exposed to light, cold, and air. He protests, screaming and gasping as he takes his first breath. His parents are thrilled, but he is less than enthusiastic about his fate, and insistently continues to search for his lost comforts and warmth.

In some ways, however, the infant's senses are remarkably prepared to help him adapt to his new life. He is endowed with a variety of potential reflex responses. He can grasp, he can kick, he can make swimming motions when on his belly, he reacts to lights and can "see," in a fashion, although he is not yet ready to understand what he sees. Recent investigations on infants reveal that within the very first days of a baby's life, he "takes in" and starts to form impressions of some things in his environment. If a toy or pencil or bright light is placed before his eyes and is slowly moved within his orbit of vision, the baby's eyes will track that object. He will even stare at complex patterns if they are put in front of him.

The newborn is quite sensitive to touch. There is some selective and protective quality about his hearing, however. While he may turn his head or respond in some manner to sounds close to him, he seems to be impervious to the sound of traffic on the street, to thunder in the sky, and to those noises in the next room or apartment that often drive his parents out of their minds. Dr. Peter H. Wolff, Professor of Psychiatry at Harvard University, who has closely studied the behavior of infants, adds that when sounds are close to them, "babies do seem to react with greater interest to such complex noises as the human voice than they do to pure tones."

The infant is, of course, sensitive to changes in temperature, and above all to touch. His handiest reflex is his ability to "root"; that is, to locate the nipple as he turns his head toward the side at which his cheek or lip has been touched. And then, to say the least, he brings with him his most vital asset, his ability to suck.

But other than arriving on the scene with these and a few other instinctive tools for adjusting to the outside world, the infant is utterly helpless in fending for himself, and he is totally dependent upon his caregivers for survival. For quite a while the infant just seems to be seeking substitute comforts for those of the womb, and for release from tensions of hunger or other bodily discomforts. If, when restless, but not too hungry or in great pain, he is held closely and gently in his mother's (or father's or whoever's) arms, he tends to quiet down. These reassuring arms, the clothes in which he is wrapped, and the warm blankets into which he is carefully tucked, approximate to some degree the security of his former life.

From now on he will be receiving his earliest samples of life and love. He will first learn about love through his body; through being touched and held and fondled and fed, through the pleasant sensations that come largely from his mouth and skin.

THE "ME" AND "THEE"

A mother's first ploys with her baby seem to result in unrequited love; as in a one-sided affair where you give and give and get little or nothing in return. As the baby makes all his unrelenting demands *heard*—if not always understood—and has them

Love Needs of the Infant

promptly attended to, he appears to be an ingrate. The only way in which he shows his appreciation to his rescuers is by merely ceasing to cry—and sometimes not even that. In fact, you could almost say the infant is a completely self-centered egoist. Except for one important point: the baby is totally unaware that he has such a thing as a self (or ego). There is no "me" or "not me" for the young infant, and there certainly is no "thee." Not sensing any boundaries, he doesn't even know where he ends and you begin. The breast or bottle or you are just further extensions of himself. To put it another way, everything is one thing. Furthermore, in his early days and weeks the baby has no way of knowing whether his discomforts arise from within his body or from the outside. Perhaps one could say that this squirming little packet of needs—who at least spends a good part of the day sleeping—is using his all to try to find relief and peace. His needs and tensions ebb and flow like the tides. There is the tension of need (hunger), and then the state of bliss (satiation). And so the cycle keeps repeating.

Isn't this state—tension, then search for release of tension—a common human experience?

During these very first weeks and months, as the baby gradually comes out of his shell, so to speak, he surely is not very discriminating. He is indifferent as to *who* fills his needs as long as these needs are filled.

Yet two things quite basic to his mental and emotional health begin to happen. Some authorities say these new developments start around the end of the first month or at the beginning of the second month, and others state these changes do not occur until around the third month. Regardless of exactly when, as the baby's needs are continuously and lovingly met—by being fed when hungry, burped gently when he has gas in his stomach, changed when he feels uncomfortably wet, held and fondled and murmured to when he feels lonely—something new takes place.

These myriad pleasant happenings that come from outside himself, and which repeat themselves, help him learn to expect and to anticipate more of the same. Through recurring little ceremonies involving body contact and pleasure, tiny impressions

The Roots of Love

and images begin to accumulate and take shape in his mind. In his dawning consciousness, he vaguely starts to connect things and somehow gets the impression that there are predictable events in his daily life. Because of this consistency, he gets a feeling that he can count on being relieved of discomfort and taken care of. Gradually, the foundations of that precious sense of trust—in himself, in people, and in things—that Erik Erikson writes of, are laid down. This feeling of trust, of knowing what to expect and to believe it will happen, is central to a person's sense of identity and security.

At the same time, the baby becomes dimly aware that the milk he receives does not flow on and on like a river. It comes to him, and then it goes away again. But it comes back too. Someone from "outside there" must be bringing him these supplies. Each time one of his other needs is satisfied, along comes that human face. The baby begins to listen for approaching footsteps. This approach alerts him: "Someone is coming to help me, to brighten up my life!" Pleasant voice nuances, certain familiar smells, tastes, and the "feel" of his mother's body as he nestles into her arms helps him realize that there is a difference between her body and his.

Alas, you are not quite "thee" just yet, since the baby will gladly accept the fond ministrations of any thee. (Do not be put off by his promiscuity. In the course of time he will single you out as that one special person who makes him the happiest and who provides him with the peak of satisfaction.) At this point in the baby's life he is just discovering that there *is* a "not me." And, utterly helpless, he feels this "other" exists only for him and for his fulfillment. She is in a way a slave; her services are taken for granted. But at this stage of development, the baby's point of view is "standard operating procedure." (Of course, the baby has no "point of view" and cannot consciously "think" such things. Right now and for a long long time to come, he is only able to *feel* and *sense* the many happenings that impinge on his existence.)

Somehow, the baby moves further away from this way of responding to life during the next few months. By the time he has had a good fill of body satisfactions (which, naturally, are never

Love Needs of the Infant

fully relinquished and continue to press for fulfillment throughout life), he will be turning toward other pleasant experiences—in the world outside his body. Occupied then with the fun of his explorations, he will be seeming to let you off the hook more often and concede, reluctantly at times, that you have a life of your own. He will be slowly recognizing the fact that you are not a slave but a person who has other interests and people to attend to. By then he will have begun to sustain a real relationship with you—which means the relationship will no longer be just one-sided.

We all, however, know people who never do seem to overcome this earlier kind of attachment behavior: that of using a person as a "need fulfilling object." We sometimes say, "He's all wrapped up in himself," and imply that such an individual sees others mostly in terms of what these others can do for him, or he does not see them at all. Relationships tend to be one-sided, people are "used" for his benefit. Sometimes such a person is demanding, greedy, selfish, or clinging. His own needs come first, and any partner who can satisfy these needs will do (and if this partner fails him in any way, he seeks another whom he expects will do better). While such behavior is appropriate for the very young infant, it will hardly do for the adult. It has been suggested that when adults relate this way to others, their emotional development may have stalled in the early months, when they did not receive their full share of devoted attention—at a time when it was basic to their emotional growth.

While we all love those who make us feel good, who gratify us—an inherent part of any love relationship—we also think of what we can do for the loved one, and how we can make him or her happy. Besides, we value the beloved person as a separate individual with unique qualities. Erich Fromm once wrote, "Immature love says, 'I love you because I need you.' Mature love says, 'I need you because I love you.'"

Admittedly, it is a long and rocky journey for us all—from infancy through adulthood—until we have reached or approximated this level of maturity.

SUBSTITUTES FOR MOTHER IN THE EARLIEST MONTHS

If the baby has not been able to tell the difference between one person and others, between one caregiver and another, does it matter if Mother leaves her baby with someone else and goes off for the day?

The answer to this question—if there is any one answer—is paradoxical. A baby benefits from getting to know and by getting used to a *few* close others from his earliest days on. However, a baby cannot be constantly handed over from one person to another like a sack of potatoes, even in these earliest weeks and months. He may become anxious as he senses the differences in handling, "handling that interrupts a familiar and expected sequence of events," as one psychiatrist has observed. Besides, babies who have to go through frequent changes in caretakers, and who cannot depend on one or two *central* figures in their lives, may have difficulties in forming close and constant attachments to others as and when they grow up. (More about this later, since this statement needs some modifications.)

In addition, says Dr. Peter Wolff, "Physical contact in the earliest months is just as important for the mother as for the child because it helps to seal the bond that establishes the mother-infant couple."

If a mother has to work, or prefers to work, even in these first months, she needs to find one responsible, loving mother substitute who is less interested in keeping Baby spotless and clean than in keeping him happy and comfortable. These substitutes may be hard to come by, and costly, but it is well worth the effort to leave no stone unturned as you search for one who can fill this bill.

Some mothers who have had to return all too soon to their jobs or careers admit they felt truly deprived of the enriching experience of becoming acquainted with their baby, of slowly establishing ties with him, and of being able to watch the exciting changes that take place in the baby almost daily. These early

Love Needs of the Infant

months are times that seem at once trying and never-ending yet precious days of pleasure that will never return. One young mother, a teacher who took time off until her baby was two years old, explained why. "I wanted to be *there* when Liza first smiled, uttered her first words, and took her first steps."

Many mothers have been able to find happy compromises by working part-time or by taking up part-time activities. They may find the intellectual and/or social stimulation for which they hunger, and manage to get out of the house for a portion of the day, but they still remain the primary figure in their baby's life and maintain this close daily relationship with him. In this way, they manage to live in the best of all possible worlds!

A sensitive mother, whatever she decides to do, or must do, will have to play this one by ear and discover for herself which choice works out best for her and her baby.

The discussion of mother-substitutes will be taken up many times during subsequent stages in the baby's life.

CUEING IN TO YOUR BABY—
THE BEGINNINGS OF COMMUNICATION

Babies and mothers are like seashells on the sands. No two are exactly alike. Just as there is no one kind of mother or mothering, there is no one kind of baby or baby way.

Each baby begins to show his own preferences of how he likes to be held and cuddled (or not cuddled), how he wants to be fed, etc. And such preferences go for Mother, too. The baby throws out signals. Mother's sensitive antennae pick up these signals, which she then responds to. And the process is reversible, too. Eventually, mother and child set up their own radar, or communications system. (And while they usually get onto the same wave length, sometimes the signals get mixed up and jammed.) This intimate exchange of signals is worked out long before words are spoken. The late Dr. D. W. Winnicott, world-famous British child psychiatrist and psychoanalyst, called this exchange "a song without words."

At first you may feel awkward and clumsy as you handle your

The Roots of Love

baby. He is quite resilient and can tolerate the possible goofs of your first attempts. Many a baby has survived a few dunkings while given his first baths, and has lived through many a pin prick while being diapered. As time goes by, you hold him comfortably, and he snuggles securely into the crook of your arm. You begin to share delights together as you laugh and play with him, as you bathe him, quiet him down, feed him. As your responses evoke responses in him—and vice versa—he catches on to what you like or do not like and tries to adjust to your ways too.

What about those days when you've had it? Those days when you are feeling tired, tense, or blue? To be sure, the baby is likely to catch your moods too, and then you may notice a change in him. Maybe he tightens up his limbs and muscles, or howls more than ever, or seems all off his schedule. But he will get over his spells just as you will. It is the overall feeling that counts, not the occasional lapses to which anyone is entitled.

One mother told her tale of woe. "There were some days and nights when Bobby was six weeks old when I really thought the world was coming to an end. Nothing went right. Fred, my husband, was down with the flu, we were cooped up in our tiny apartment, Mother and Dad were divorcing, our older child, age two, was jealous of the baby and making trouble, and I was exhausted, mentally, physically and emotionally. Bobby screamed so much at times he couldn't even take notice of the nipple near his mouth although he was hungry. And, to clinch matters, he began to cry soon after he was fed. Although we later found he had had some sort of colic, I thought at that time my tensions had ruined him forever!" Happily, things picked up again for this mother, her problems and anxiety subsided, and except for the baby's unpredictable episodes of colic, he bounced back to his usual easygoing self again.

The cueing in that starts now is the very beginning of communication. It will develop later on into a special capacity to listen with your heart as well as your ears to what your child is trying to tell you and his father. This close "listening" to expressions, body movements, and feeling tones as the child

Love Needs of the Infant

speaks or cries out his problems—taking note of his silences, too—will also encourage him to listen to you. He is more likely then to also "hear" your guiding words and to listen to the instructions you will be giving him as he grows older—and which you will expect him to understand and follow. But even now, before words are known to him, he will catch your inflections, your real meanings.

In the early stages of the baby's life, parents communicate with him primarily through feeding, through responding to the baby's cry, through their own way of "talking" to him, and through smiling. And the baby communicates in his way through these experiences, too.

FEEDING AND LOVE: BABY DOTH NOT LIVE BY MILK ALONE

Who isn't glad to eat when hungry? Yet eating by oneself is not nearly as enjoyable as eating and sharing food in agreeable company. Small wonder that food and love are so often equated, as in the expressions "I could eat her up" or "He is starved for love." Food is usually the ritual around which festivities are celebrated, when goodwill and warm feelings flow as abundantly as the meal—prepared and served with love and care.

A man and woman in love, a husband and wife wishing to rekindle the spark and romance of their marital relationship, and even people transacting business often choose to dine or lunch out in a pleasant atmosphere, with a drink or with wine, and (it is hoped) with tasty food served up in an appetizing manner. If no one is rushed, the outside pressures may be forgotten for a while. The good feelings that come with filling an empty stomach, along with the human interchanges, make the whole experience relaxing and emotionally—as well as physically—nourishing. Even a cup of coffee and a doughnut shared with our neighbors, friends, or relatives will create a genial climate for communication and goodwill.

This food ritual counts even more for the baby. As Dr. Peter B. Neubauer, Director of the Child Development Center in New

The Roots of Love

York City and Clinical Professor of Psychiatry, Downstate Medical Center, New York, points out, "To the same degree that nutritive values are important to the baby's physical health, the experiences *around* feeding are important to his mental health." Besides obtaining relief from hunger and the satisfaction of his natural urge to suck, the baby needs "contact comfort" with another human being. Baby does not live by milk alone.

The famous monkeys studied by Dr. Harry H. Harlow, Professor of Psychology at the University of Wisconsin, have shown us a lot about feeding, comforting, and communication. He and his associates took a group of baby rhesus monkeys and put them into a cage with two kinds of surrogate "mothers." One type was made of wire and topped with a wooden head and face, while the other was identical, except that "she" was covered with a soft terry cloth. A few of the monkey babies were fed by the wire mother, and a few were fed by the terry-cloth mother. Regardless of the fact that both mothers provided milk, the two groups of monkeys would run over to the terry-cloth figure to cuddle and cling to. When they were frightened or under stress, all monkeys rushed to her. While near the terry-cloth mother, the monkeys showed more interest in exploring their environment, as well as more daring.

(Sadly enough, although the monkeys did receive the warmth and cuddly sensations they needed, the lack of communication, stimulation, and interaction that goes on between a real monkey mother and her baby proved to be a serious handicap in their social and emotional development. The monkeys became unsociable and sometimes antisocial as well when allowed to mingle with peers. They tended to be withdrawn, and often would sit gazing into space. At other times, some of the monkeys with pseudomothers would attack others, or even attack themselves by pulling out their hair and tearing at their skin. Finally, they had difficulties in their sexual development and ability to mate.)

Now back to humans again. The first question about feeding that comes to the minds of many mothers is, "Shall I breast-feed or bottle-feed my baby? Which will mean the most for his present and future emotional development?"

Love Needs of the Infant

If a mother wants to and is able to breast-feed her baby, the experience can be deeply satisfying to her and to her child. The baby is in close proximity with his mother's body and her warm skin, and the mother too receives pleasant body sensations from the nursing, as well as emotional pleasure. During these moments—if all goes well with the breast-feeding itself—mother and child may seem almost to merge in complete enjoyment of each other.

Somehow it is a less happy and rewarding experience if a mother nurses merely because she thinks she "ought" to—because she believes intellectually that breast-feeding is essential to good mothering. Far more important than breast or bottle is the heart that goes with it. A bottle-fed baby can receive many of the same benefits if he is held close to his mother and feels the warmth and protectiveness of her body and arms. Much research has shown that what counts is the degree of intimacy and rapport that bind mother and infant together during these moments.

Anne Richardson Roiphe, who so well understands a harassed young mother's conflicts between wanting to give her baby the best of herself and wanting a personal life of her own, writes in her book, *Up the Sandbox*, of the mother's delights in feeding her baby:

> And with each feeding, each soothing, each moment we live together, I grow into him. My spirit oozes out, I feel myself contracting and him expanding, and the ties between us solidify.

As discussed in the previous chapter, these feeding times are the times during which a mother—quite unaware—may give out much of herself to her baby, just as she was given to as an infant. Or, not having had sufficient mothering, she may do for the baby what she wishes could have been done for her. As she feels what her baby needs, and what *she* may have needed—offering the best of herself—she may replenish and nourish her inner self simultaneously.

"It takes two to tango," and in this dance (or any dance involving close body contact) the partners have to be in step with each other. If there is an occasional stumble or two, an adjustment is made, and the pair soon pick up their timing once more. After a while the leader gets to know how to lead this particular partner, who in turn learns how to follow, even while indicating subtly the variations she enjoys the best. The two "feel" each other's steps, which become unison in harmony and rhythm. Their mutual pleasure is intense.

But all is not fun and games. Feeding can be discouraging—to understate—when the baby turns his head away from you, shuts his mouth tight, shoves the nipple away, spits out his food, falls asleep, cries, or kicks you in the stomach! Like other mothers, you may feel the baby is rejecting you or your handling. Convinced this is so, you may begin to have sinking doubts about your talents as a mother. Needless to say, your doubts are likely to be unfounded. Your baby may just be telling you that for some reason he has a bellyache, is tired, or has had enough. A number of nutritionists and pediatricians are becoming more and more convinced that many babies in this country are overfed—that is, provided they are able to *get* enough proper nourishment. And yet here we are, overly anxious about getting in every single ounce and calorie.

FEEDINGS AND ATTITUDES TOWARD LIFE

A mother and baby who do not hit it off perfectly during mealtimes sometimes find their greatest mutual pleasure during play or bath time, or through other happily shared moments. Feedings, however, offer the pair so many opportunities to know each other, communicate, and establish deep bonds, that they have often been studied as reflections of the total relationship between mother and child.

One such study conducted on 131 children from the time of birth up to their seventh year suggests that many values inherent in the feeding sessions relate, to a great extent, to the child's future mental health. Films were taken of these babies and their mothers during feedings, starting at six weeks, then again at six months, and finally at one year of age. The researchers, Dr.

Love Needs of the Infant

Sylvia Brody, Adjunct Professor of Psychology, Graduate Center of the City University of New York, and Dr. Sidney Axelrad, Dean of Graduate Studies at Queens College of the City University of New York, discovered some amazing things when the babies were given psychological tests at the end of their first year. They noted that those babies who had had pleasurable mealtime experiences showed a much greater capacity to wait, to concentrate, to learn, to solve problems, and to anticipate and expect pleasure from people and things than did the babies who had experienced anxieties and tensions during their feedings. However, as Dr. Brody remarked, "We have found that it is the *repeated* good or unhappy feedings that mattered and not the occasional interference such as teething, fatigue, time of day, recent or incipient illness, family stress, or even the weather, that may keep the feeding from being emotionally satisfying."

Through having had both physical and emotional needs adequately met, the babies who tested well showed their growing interest in the world outside their bodies. They fitted pegs into pegboards, put cubes into containers, and tried to find the object that was hidden behind a screen. They showed pleasure when they succeeded, but not too much disappointment when they failed. The babies whose feedings had not been happy showed less ability to concentrate, and were impatient with or indifferent to the objects, either pushing them aside or just mouthing them.

Dr. Brody goes on to say that the babies' own constitutional factors and their individual personalities were also taken into account as their feeding sessions were observed. Some babies were more irritable, other more lethargic, some sensitive to or negative about certain foods. "However," she continued, "we have seen irritable, highstrung babies become relaxed and calmed through feedings that are quiet and enjoyable, and we have also seen 'easy' babies become 'difficult' through continuous mother-child battles during the meals."

The researchers were looking for the specific attitudes that seemed to make mealtimes an enjoyable event for all. Did a mother permit her baby to take some initiative during the feeding, even though she still took the lead? This meant, was a

The Roots of Love

mother allowing her baby to pause, if he so wished, and stretch out his limbs, touch her face or breast with his hands, look around, push the bottle or breast away when he had had enough? And, when he grew a bit older, did she encourage his self-feeding with solids, messy as this might be? Could a mother help her baby wait for his food by reassuring him, perhaps by the tone of her voice, that food would be forthcoming? Some mothers carried their baby with them as they prepared the food, or placed him in a position where the baby could watch the food being prepared. Others might hand the baby a spoon to remind him that mealtime was approaching. All of these tactics seem also to help the baby turn his attention from his inner (body) self out toward the world around him.

Among some of the other attitudes Drs. Brody and Axelrad searched for was flexibility. Was a mother flexible enough to try something else if what she was doing during the feeding did not seem to work? As an example, would she follow her baby's cues when he kicked or cried or arched his back stiffly, trying to convey to her the message that he did *not* want to be burped at that moment, he did *not* want his solids, but rather, "Please, let us get on with my milk"?

The babies in this study have now become children beginning grade school. Dr. Brody and her staff have good evidence to indicate that each child's emotional, intellectual, and social development reflect the patterns established between mother and child during his first year of life. Nevertheless, Dr. Brody stresses, "Experiences of the early months are *not* irreversible." For instance, a colicky baby can catch up and blossom once the difficulty has subsided. (And more about colicky babies later.)

Another psychologist, Dr. Lois B. Murphy, Director of Child Research at the Menninger Foundation in Topeka, Kansas, has also concluded from several studies on babies and small children that satisfying early feeding experiences result in babies "whose response to many aspects of life later carries the qualities of zestful feelings that 'life tastes good.' "

And now for another form of communication: the cry.

Love Needs of the Infant

THE MEANINGS OF THE BABY'S CRIES

"Let him cry it out!" "It's good exercise for his lungs!" "He's just crying for attention, leave him alone!" These were the old adages and advice given to many parents of previous generations, and, sadly enough, still given today by many of those brought up under such a spartan regime. ("What was good enough for me is good enough for you!")

Now it is known that a baby's cry has a meaning which deserves to be understood.

Obviously, before a baby knows how to talk, his cry is his first form of communication, his primary effort to express himself. Certainly he is trying to get attention that he needs, and he achieves this through vocalizing. Bit by bit he discovers that his SOS brings a human response; a person arrives along with the relief. These responses to his cries give him confidence that distress is always followed by some kind of soothing, and that by his own efforts he can make an impact upon his environment. It is said that fairly prompt relief of distress leads later in life to an optimistic and challenging feeling that by using appropriate means, difficulties can be overcome. (Perhaps here is the origin of that expression "You will *hear* from that young man [or woman] someday!")

In observing the development of twenty-six infant-mother pairs over a period of a year, Dr. Mary D. Salter Ainsworth, Professor of Psychology, and Dr. Silvia M. Bell, Department of Child Psychiatry, both at Johns Hopkins School of Medicine, came up with striking evidence in favor of what some may consider "spoiling" the child (and more about spoiling later). They noted that despite varying degrees of constitutional differences in irritability in babies, when a mother responded promptly and consistently to her infant's cries, the baby tended to cry very little—both in duration and frequency—by the end of the first year. Whereas, "those infants who are conspicuous for fussing and crying after the first few months of life and who fit

The Roots of Love

the stereotype of the 'spoiled child' are those whose mothers have ignored their cries or have delayed in responding to them." The researchers also noticed that toward the end of their first year, the responded-to babies had become more independent and were more able to use means other than crying to get their mothers' attention.

Should the baby's crying be *repeatedly* ignored, he is apt to become discouraged at his efforts and may lose confidence in the expectations of a gratifying return. He may tend to withdraw much of his energy from the outside world and "give up," so to speak.

In adulthood, when no one pays attention to our efforts—perhaps repeating a pattern established and fixed in our mind since infancy and early childhood—our discouragement makes it increasingly difficult to communicate and establish contact with others. We may become inhibited and find it hard to make our real feelings and needs known. Communicating is basic to the art of loving, through which one partner expresses his love for the other and is able to tell the loved one how he feels, even if at times these feelings are not the happiest.

Now, this does not mean a baby should never be left to cry. One mother proudly but unwisely commented, "I don't wait for Tommy to cry. I get there *before* he cries!" Jumping into the act instantly every time you hear a whimper may deprive the baby of the need to make any efforts on his part, just as letting him cry endlessly can squelch these efforts. (Of course, there are babies who hardly ever cry. Some of them are just placid and easygoing by nature and/or suffer little from tugging pains or sensitive needs. Yet sometimes these very "good" babies are deceptively quiet and undemanding, and could benefit from attention even if they do not *seem* to need it.)

And what about the cry itself? How does one get to know what the baby wants?

It may be helpful to understand that even if you run to your baby's rescue fairly promptly and feed him when all he needs is to be burped, or burp him when he needs to be fed, or change his diapers when all he wants is to be held, he senses at least that

Love Needs of the Infant

someone hears him and is trying to give him some assistance. It is quite possible then, as time goes by, that his code of transmitting signals will become more distinct and his human partner will be able to decode them more accurately.

Sooner or later, a mother begins to distinguish the hunger cry from the shrill, piercing cry of pain—as in colic, when a baby may simultaneously pull up or stretch his limbs, or arch his back. She gets to know when her baby is just overtired, or wants to go to sleep but cannot seem to make it. Perhaps he yells for a few minutes, or cries *sotto voce* a little while before dropping off to sleep. You may find it disconcerting if your baby cries while he is being undressed. Am I holding him the wrong way? you may wonder, when all he may be crying about is losing the warmth and sense of bodily security as his clothes are being removed. Gentle ministrations of one kind or other for a few moments may help him quickly overcome this feeling of "sudden shock."

More often than not, some babies just feel lonely. They want to be held, to have close contact with whoever is tending to them. Sometimes a baby cries again after he has been put down because he has not received the quota of love necessary to reassure him; or because, finding it hard to stop the fun he has had before you put him down in his crib, he wants to be patted and talked to gently for a little while. As a baby gets to be a little older, he may want company, a change of scene; he might enjoy sitting up (or being inclined in a baby seat) to see what is going on around him, and he may cry because at the moment there is no other way to tell you this.

And just at the point where you are sure you know what his cries are all about, and you could tell him proudly if he'd understand, "I can read you now!" off he goes into a crying spell, and nothing you do seems to stop it. You have even checked for symptoms of illness.

Even though every little whimper has a meaning of its own, you may not *always* know what that meaning is. The important thing is whether the baby stops reasonably soon or whether his crying continues and builds up. If it builds up, you try your best to comfort him—and that is all you can do.

Colicky Babies

Only parents who have had a colicky baby know what it is like: endless days *and* nights of picking up the shrieking, hurting baby, of holding him, walking him, of trying to soothe and distract him, or turning him into different positions—all of which places a tremendous strain on parents. They feel so helpless, especially when nothing they do seems to help. The constant crying may drive a parent up the wall, and then she or he is apt to feel guilty for harboring resentful thoughts and feelings ("If only we could have *one* night of unbroken sleep!"), and furthermore, they both may be dissatisfied with themselves for not being able to "do" anything to change the miserable situation.

Yet, as many of these same parents have discovered, to their well-deserved joy, once the baby is over his gastric discomforts—which sometimes may not be until his third or fourth month, or later—he often blossoms out into an especially alert, responsive, active, and gurgling child. But why? No one seems to know exactly, but there is some speculation among several child-care experts that all the extra holding, soothing, and stimulating the baby received in these first months contributed to the advanced and enriched development of his personality. And, as some parents have said, "As soon as the pain has stopped, he just wants to live it up!"

In the meantime, there are a variety of soothing aids that parents of all babies who are restless may want to try out. These will be discussed in the following chapter.

THE BABY'S SMILE

Some of us can remember from our own childhood how a loving smile or an understanding look saved the day for us during a scary experience. Messages are passed between lovers through intimate looks and knowing smiles. And we are won over by the person who greets us with an open smile that includes the upper part of the face. The person whose mouth moves mechanically into a smile but whose eyes remain silent and cannot light up is a "dead pan."

Love Needs of the Infant

In our everyday conversations, in idiomatic expressions, we will say, "She's the apple of her father's eye," "You're sure a sight for sore eyes," and we know that "The eyes are the windows of the soul." Ben Jonson's sentimental "Drink to me only with thine eyes and I will pledge with mine" and the song "When Irish Eyes Are Smiling" tell us how much facial expressions set a tone for most of our human communications and transactions, which get their start in early infancy.

In his very youngest days of what Grandma might call the "gas smile," the baby is actually responding along reflex lines to a number of stimuli. According to Dr. Peter Wolff, a reflex or spontaneous smile can be evoked "on order" by stroking a baby's cheek or belly, or by cooing at him. In addition, a gentle upward pull of his mouth can be seen sometimes during or after a contented feeding. Soon, these reactions begin to take on a more definite meaning.

Through eye-to-eye contact with his mother or mother-figure, through seeing pleasant sights and hearing pleasant sounds, the baby's capacity to smile begins to grow. As his eyes first start to focus, a baby will sometimes try to follow his mother's figure as she enters the room. (He may even smile in response to her voice as early as the third or fourth week of life.)

While his mother looks down and smiles at him as she gives the breast or bottle, the baby's gaze may gradually shift from these objects to search the upper part of her face. Following this, the eyes of mother and child fix on each other. Then suddenly, at some odd moment—perhaps during a feeding—the baby may stop sucking, stare at her, and give her a wide, happy, toothless grin.

At last a mother receives her long-due reward, and she feels her baby is finally showing his appreciation. Everything—all the fussing, fretting, crying, the difficult times—seems to vanish like the memory of labor.

The appearance of this smile, called the "social smile," can be seen as early as the end of the first month to as late as the end of the third month, or even at the beginning of the fourth month.

The Roots of Love

Some mothers claim their babies smiled at them—and not in reflex either—during the end of the third *week*.

A young mother had her month-old baby girl stretched out on her knees. Holding her arms and looking her in the eye, the mother bent over and talked gibberish to her infant. The infant's arms and legs immediately went into excited action. She stared at her mother, smiling almost ecstatically, then pushed forward her neck and gurgled strenuously as if she were trying to tell her mother something, too.

An infant is inclined to smile sooner when there are other people milling about and talking to him. Often a playful brother or sister will get a smile out of him. Some babies smile more brightly, others more shyly. And still others are not such "smileys" but may be good observers of life: serious, reflective, intent on the objects surrounding them to which they react with obvious interest. One might say that right now they are "things people" rather than "people people." But this attitude often changes later on when the baby has learned to talk.

As has been said before, from two months to four or five months, the baby does all he can to win attention—from everyone. His smile, when it comes, can be so utterly disarming and contagious, even to the most hard-bitten adult, that you may feel some disappointment when you realize this smile is not yet reserved for you or his father.

In a way, however, all faces do mean "Mother" to him, since he cannot tell at this stage of development that people have different faces. *His smile at others is really a smile for you,* to show his gratitude that you are always there when he needs you. It will not be long now before he is able to tell you apart from the others in his life, and his smile for you will be very special then. And later in life, his warm smile will be a calling card: an introduction to others and a human-relations aid.

The adoring look and smile that are exchanged between mother and child are also recaptured later in adulthood between lovers. Selma Fraiberg, Professor of Child Psychoanalysis, University of Michigan Medical Center, writes so aptly:

> During the first six months the baby has rudiments of a love language; there is the language of the smile, the language of vocal

Love Needs of the Infant

sound-making, the language of the embrace. It's the essential vocabulary of love before we can yet speak of love . . . when the baby is grown up and "falls in love" for the first time, he will woo his partner through the language of the smile, through the utterance of endearments and the joy of the embrace.

CHAPTER FOUR

Soothing, Stimulating, and Spoiling

There is an infinite number of ways of soothing a crying infant's miseries, some of which can make life generally pleasanter, easier, and more fun for all. There are also different ways in which to stimulate him, to help him become more responsive to the people and things in his environment. Even more important, the very nature of the more intimate and personal experiences that will be described are apt to strengthen the emotional bonds between parents and child.

One individual baby may take to one of the suggested forms of soothing, while another may resist. You too may find one or several of these aids more enjoyable, others less so. For example, to repeat, most babies love to be cuddled, but a few prefer to be held only lightly. Such babies may dislike the feeling of being restrained, of having their movements restricted. They will show this by wriggling or squirming, pushing away from whoever holds them, or by crying as they are held close. This resistance seems to be built-in and has little to do with Mother's skill in handling her baby. Some of these babies love to be kissed, to have their faces and skin stroked and patted, and to be bounced gently. They love motion too, as do all babies, but want to keep their muscles going.

Therefore, as you read on, see what suits you and your baby the best. Pick and choose.

Soothing, Stimulating, and Spoiling
SOOTHING

The Cradle
Baby, seven weeks old, was crying in the crib. Mother, having tried everything, was frantic. Father, meanwhile, was watering the potted plants in the antique cradle adorning the living room. What is wrong with this picture?

Once upon a time, the cradle rocked prince and pauper alike. Its friendly companion, the rocking chair, was close at its side. But one dark Victorian night, they both disappeared. A wicked witch banished them from the nursery and turned them into decorators' items!

The late Dr. René Spitz, psychiatrist of international fame, suggested that the infant under the age of three or four months is unable to discharge his tensions through active body movements and needs some help. (As mentioned earlier, these tensions can be other than just hunger: they may be gastric distress, restlessness, fatigue, etc.) In other days, Dr. Spitz noted, methods of helping Baby—which now have become the subject of scorn—were known to every mother. "Our grandmothers also knew that if you rock the infant he will become quiet and go quietly to sleep," he said. "Nevertheless, we have discarded the cradle, and I know of no valid reasons for doing so."

No doubt Dr. Spitz was referring to the great-grandmothers of today's young parents, because the cradle and rocking chair were on their way out as early as the 1890s. In 1879, Mark Twain mentioned "the three or four million cradles now rocking in the land." And a poet still dared to write, "Like a cradle rocking, rocking/Silent, peaceful, to and fro." But soon, toward the end of the nineteenth century, both cradle and rocker were blacklisted by pediatricians. Child-care literature warned mothers that rocking was a "vicious practice," "folly," "evil," "injurious to the nerves," and Dr. L. Emmett Holt, a well-known pediatrician of that era—the Dr. Spock of his day—declared, "rocking and all other habits of this sort may be harmful." A mother's manual of 1916 advised that cradles were "harmful equipment . . . that

The Roots of Love

have no place in a baby nursery." By the mid-twenties, the cradle had long been thought to be an invention of the devil, or at least hopelessly old-fashioned.

At last, in the thirties, one lone pediatrician bravely suggested that gentle swaying motions could soothe a baby's "excited nervous system," and could help young digestions, referring to "dyspeptic" babies, presently called "colicky" babies. And now the pendulum has begun to swing once again with the cradle and rocker, which can be seen here and there as nursery furniture in department stores. (A recently advertised model is a lucite cradle that can be rocked by a motor-mother!)

Don't many of us daydream sometimes of a peaceful summer afternoon when we can lie gently swaying in a hammock with a favorite book in our laps and a cool drink by our sides? Dr. Samuel Berenberg, Associate Professor of Pediatrics, Cornell University Medical Center, New York, who keeps a cradle in his office, is always amazed at how many little girls and boys get the message that dolls should be rocked to sleep in it. "It seems almost intuitive," the doctor says, "since most of the children have never seen a cradle before."

The doctors who favor the cradle all seem to agree that rocking should be a nonexhaustive activity, conducive to relaxation, that is transmitted from parent to child. This is quite another thing from the frenetic jiggling and joggling of baby carriages that one often sees in parks and playgrounds. That kind of bouncing and jiggling can be overwhelming and overstimulating to a baby. Rather, it is a fluid, gentle quality of rocking that does the soothing. One psychologist adds that a tiny baby is helped to feel secure when he can fit into such a snug little place. Furthermore, as he gets to be a bit older, he can see his mother's face through the open slats in the cradle, making this one more source of pleasure and comfort to him.

Despite the past unpopularity of cradles, some parents who handed them down, unabashed, to succeeding generations can vouch for their important place in the family. Other parents, knowing that a crib will soon have to replace the cradle, object solely on the basis of financial considerations. And one young

Soothing, Stimulating, and Spoiling

mother stated bluntly, "Who wants to bend over so far when you have to pick up the baby fifty times a day?" Still other parents feel that all the pros outweigh the cons and believe the investment well worth it, all the more since they can usually sell the cradle to others once it has outlived its usefulness. Or, they often can borrow one from a friend or relative, and lend theirs too.

The Rocking Chair

The rocker can serve a dual purpose. Your own maternal or paternal tensions may be soothed by collapsing, when exhausted, into this welcoming resting place, if only for ten minutes at a time. And if Baby is crying or fretting, take him along too. As you kick the shoes off your tired feet and settle into the rocker, putting a pillow under the arm that holds your baby (or holding him like a kitten on your shoulder), you may find the experience equivalent to several group encounter sessions! By letting go and unwinding during these moments of repose, you may accomplish two things. You may be able to tune in on another, more tranquil wave length, and as you feel the warm little body of your baby respond to the rocking and perhaps to your gentle patting or stroking of his back—if you feel this helps—you may sense an increase in your ability to express your own tender and affectionate feelings.

Dr. Berenberg says, "When a mother rocks a baby in her arms or on her shoulder, we really don't know whether it is the closeness of the mother or the rocking motion that soothes the baby. We do know that rhythmic motion has always seemed to make babies happy. They love the motion of cars and, as they get older, of swings, see-saws and rocking-horses."

"Won't all this rocking become a habit?" asked one concerned young father. The answers given by several child-care experts could be summed up in brief: Any practice in infancy can become a "habit" that is hard to break, be it breast-feeding, bottle-feeding, the use of a pacifier, you name it. This does not mean the practice is bad. It does mean that it is being used in the wrong way for the wrong reasons. Perhaps this idea can be crystallized by explaining that all of these practices are resorted to for a reason: to feed the baby, to soothe the fretting infant, and to give him what he needs. However, if these measures are carried on past the time when the baby is in need of such help, for instance, when the baby has shown he is happy drinking from a cup and shows he doesn't miss his bottle, then one might call continuing the bottle as promoting a "habit." Nevertheless, there may be times of stress, illness, or fatigue, even when the baby has become a toddler, when he may want to be held and rocked, and can well benefit from this comforting.

More Motion

As fathers who have spent hours walking the baby around the house at night well know, motion does seem to have a soporific effect on restless and "hurting" infants. For many centuries—and in cultures less sophisticated than ours—babies have been carried about on parental backs, or on hips, in cradle boards or in slings. Many modern parents also have discovered the advantages of taking their babies with them whenever they can by carrying them in canvas slings, and, when the infants can hold their heads up, they often hoist the babies into a back pack. The baby enjoys not only the motion but the physical contact with his parent. Besides, in a very pleasant way, he gets a chance to see and know the world at a different angle from that of the crib.

Some parents find their babies will settle down as soon as they are in a carriage, or a car or bus. Other parents swear by the baby bouncer, which they use for short periods during the day, after the baby has reached three or four months of age. At this time, as with the back pack, the child is in full view of his environment, and while he happily bounces and exercises his limbs, he can watch Mother and all of her busyness.

While no one knows for sure just why gentle rockings, swayings, and other motions do comfort and soothe, Dr. Esmond Morris, ethologist and author, suggests that these motions (particularly those that include holding the baby close to one's body) may recreate the soft, swaying motions the baby felt when

Soothing, Stimulating, and Spoiling

inside his mother's womb. But regardless of why, these measures seem to work.

Touch

In some of the Mediterranean and Latin countries, where emotions are apt to be volatile and comparatively free, one will see men embracing and kissing each other passionately as they greet, congratulate, or say farewell to each other. They are apt to have few hangups about touching one another or displaying warm and spontaneous feelings. Emotions tend to be far more controlled in Anglo-Saxon countries. In our own nation, perhaps some bars are let down during New Year's Eve, or during football games when after a touchdown players and spectators will cheer and yell and throw their arms about each other, kissing in joyous excitement. But otherwise we more or less tend to keep our distance. One of the reasons may be that we are afraid the display of any physical affection or contact will be interpreted as sexual, particularly with a member of the same sex.

Surely there are other grounds for being so uptight and inhibited about demonstrating genuine feeling through physical contact in public—and sometimes in private too. And all of this despite the deep human need and longing for closeness and intimacy. While everyone knows that touching and being touched are part of the joy of life and the feeling of being alive, some persons remain forever "touch hungry," yet dare not reach out. Our very words betray these sometimes unconscious longings as we say, "You can pat me on the back," "I was so touched by your thought," "His performance *held* me!" "Let us keep in touch," and much more.

An artist who illustrated many children's books was able to do imaginative drawings of animals, inanimate objects, and children in action. Yet this artist, who had had a cold, remote father, was never able to get the feel of a father's physical involvement with his youngsters. In one illustration where Daddy has just picked up his three-year-old, the Daddy's arms are stretched out rigidly at right angles in front of him, and the child's body hangs down stiffly and lifelessly quite some inches away from his father's body.

It is more than likely that the baby's future capacity to express tenderness can be fostered through the various soothing, tactile sensations experienced now. The baby absorbs these sensations like a sponge. They tell him he is loved. And later, in adulthood, he also "tells" his beloved she is loved—not only through his words of endearment, but through his touch.

In a pilot study conducted at the State University medical center in Buffalo, New York, nurses and aides were instructed to gently handle and stroke five premature babies inside their incubators for five minutes every hour during their first ten days of life. The babies who had been caressed were more active and gained weight more rapidly than five other control infants who had not received this special attention. After seven months, a pediatrician who had no knowledge of the experiment examined all ten babies. He found that the handled infants were all developing normally, but that only one of the other group was doing as well.

This does not mean that parents who have "preemies" need to be alarmed if their infants were not fondled when in incubators. Their babies may also flourish under warm and tender care once they have left the hospital. It is quite possible too that the control babies did not receive their proper share of fondling after they returned home. Yet the fact that the first group did develop more rapidly under the special attention they received gives one much to ponder.

Here are some other ways through which the baby receives happy tactile impressions:

THE BATH. An ad reads, "Touch is a baby's ear . . . touch more than talk is what a baby best understands." The surface of an infant's skin is as sensitive as it is soft. This delicate skin responds to the warm rays of the sun, to a cool breeze on a hot day, and to the caressing water of his bath.

The "daily" bath counts more for happiness than for hygiene. (And if you have to skip it for several days when you are up to

Soothing, Stimulating, and Spoiling

your neck in chores or demands on you, no harm done to health *or* happiness.) At the same time, the more a baby can learn to expect certain regular events—and this need not be the bath event—the more he builds up a feeling of "good things happen to me." *I* must be "good." This bathing ritual is another source of mutual delight for Mother and Baby—or Father and Baby. Although some infants may resist at first (and it helps to immerse the infant gently, beginning with his feet and then the buttocks, following slowly with the rest of his body) most babies get to love the feel of the warm water touching their skin. And why not? Surely the baby must "remember" in some way his days of having been surrounded by fluid as he was carried in his mother's womb. The lightness of the water helps the baby kick out his tiny legs. He makes swimming motions, in a plastic tub or kitchen sink, whether being held on his back or front. Sometimes a baby will coo and babble with joy as he kicks out. The feel of the soft towel and cozy sensation of a nice clean diaper and fresh clothes add to the fun.

The baby's good body feelings help him form a healthy image of his own body self, and, as he begins to touch his fingers and his toes, he learns more about what belongs to him and what belongs to the "other." Besides, all these pleasant sensations are associated with Mother, or whoever brings them to him, and they strengthen his growing ties to her. Gradually then, in later months, the focus of his enjoyment begins to shift from his own body to his mother, who has done all these good things for and with him.

"SWADDLING." Since touch is also a tranquilizer, parents in many countries and cultures have soothed their babies through an overall form of touching called "swaddling." The swaddled baby is tightly bound up in a blanket in such a way that his arms and legs are immobilized. Most of our Western society has looked askance on swaddling, but some recent observations made on newborns have shown rather startling results that have caused many to take a new look at the old custom.

These observations indicated that swaddled babies slept more, cried less, and had lower heartbeat rates than did the other babies. Yet infants never swaddled before would not tolerate this restriction if it was attempted at two or three months of life, a time when babies need *lebensraum* to stretch and exercise their limbs. Some doctors now believe that if all else has failed and a very young infant will not cease crying, his cries may be lessened through the application of a moderate version of swaddling, provided the infant does not strongly resist. The restless baby then can be wrapped up securely and snugly in a warm blanket, and while his body is being gently embraced all over by this firm covering, he is given slack to permit him some degree of motion. After all, the baby was sufficiently free to kick around a bit even in his mother's womb.

Sucking

The baby gets his first taste of the world and its goodness as he satisfies both his hunger and thirst, as well as his basic need to suck. For reasons that are not very clear, the sucking drive varies in babies, from very strong to relatively mild. (Some babies have had practice at sucking before birth. Photographs clearly show these babies having a go at their thumbs in utero.) You will notice one infant avidly attacking and gulping down his milk, while another takes it at a more moderate pace, and another dawdles or even falls asleep over his bottle or at the breast.

Dr. Lois Murphy comments, "Sucking is the first effort to earn a living, or to work, and for some involves considerable struggle or requires considerable encouragement . . ." At times, a baby will go after his milk so fast that after the milk is all gone he keeps right on sucking his fingers, or perhaps the corner of a blanket or anything else near him. (Your doctor or clinic nurse can tell you whether your baby is drinking too fast or not fast enough, and how to remedy this.)

After the baby has taken *in* the world through his mouth, he begins to reach *out* toward the world, but still via his mouth. He starts to mouth objects, and later, when he is able to grasp with purpose, he often puts anything he can get hold of into his mouth. It feels so good—to him at least—and at the same time he is testing the shape and texture of things.

Soothing, Stimulating, and Spoiling

Later on in life, when man and woman kiss, the mouth again becomes a part of the body that receives (and gives) great pleasure.

Thumbs

And what is more convenient and accessible to suck on than his thumb? Fortunately, we've come a long way from the dark ages in baby care when parents tied the baby's hands down onto the mattress, put mittens or bandages on them, or daubed his thumb with bitter medicine. Even so, some parents still get an uncomfortable feeling when they first notice that thumb in Baby's mouth, and they worry, "We've got a thumb-sucker!" These uncomfortable feelings may be related in part to similar long-forgotten prohibitions given us by our parents years ago, and which now are recalled in some obscure way.

Dentists reassure us that thumb-sucking is not likely to affect the shape of teeth or jaw unless it is continued to the time of the appearance of permanent teeth. Mental-health experts reassure us that thumb-sucking—if not resorted to all the time—satisfies a baby's normal need. Thumb-sucking may be at first a part of the sucking need. Later it becomes a comforter, a substitute for Mother and nipple, used more frequently at bedtime, when the baby is tired, or when he is anxious or not feeling up to par.

Just as some babies never do seek their thumbs, others continue to thumb-suck throughout the first year, and still others only relinquish this prop at some point during their first three years of life. Many young children turn back to it under stresses and strains.

Maybe we can be more sympathetic with and tolerant of Baby's mouth and sucking pleasures if we remind ourselves of how many of us find solace and comfort in a drink, cigarette, stick of gum, sweet, or snack when things seem rough going—when we are tense and when our relationships with people seem to have gone awry. But we also know today that when any of these soothers become excesses, they may point to an earlier emotional or body need that was either curtailed too soon or prolonged.

The Roots of Love

Typically, as the baby becomes more taken by the people and things surrounding him, the need for his thumb usually diminishes.

Pacifier

A few generations ago, the pacifier was looked upon with horror by parents and doctors alike. Today the pacifier is neither favored or frowned upon, depending, of course, on how it is used.

Although nearly anything goes that will soothe the discomforts of a tiny baby, especially a colicky one, there are parents who found the pacifier so useful in their baby's early weeks that they come to rely upon it as he gets older. You often see a mother pop a pacifier into the mouth of her fretting baby who is old enough to stand or even walk—without trying to find out what is really bothering him.

One mother who had mixed feelings about pacifiers looked at their use in this way: "When Tony was about three or four weeks old, he had long crying spells that nearly drove us crazy. Since we had done all we could, we decided to give him a pacifier, and he miraculously quieted down. We could never understand just why. The pacifier would automatically drop out of his mouth while he was asleep, and we only gave it to him sparingly. After a few weeks of whatever ailed him, that pacifier just disappeared from our lives and was never missed."

Often a baby will push out his pacifier after he is about four months old. He can put in his thumb now if he so wishes, and take it out too, all on his own.

By and large, doctors feel it is wise to discourage the use of the pacifier after the baby's first months—at a time when he is more apt to react to and enjoy the various stimulations that come from outside of his self.

Sound

Unfortunately, in many homes the lullabye went out with the cradle. Today's harassed mothers often cannot find the time, while others feel self-conscious about singing to their babies before bedtime, and still others do not know any lullabyes and

Soothing, Stimulating, and Spoiling

are not aware that *any* tune will do, rock included! Yet the human voice always has helped to calm babies who are irritable. And we already know the baby will turn his head early in life when he hears a sound nearby, and soon, when hungry, will stop crying at hearing a voice, particularly when he hears his mother's voice.

Dr. Lee Salk, Clinical Professor of Psychology and Pediatrics, Cornell University Medical College, New York, tells us that amplified regular heartbeat sounds were relayed to babies in a hospital nursery during the first days of their lives with such good results that they cried less and gained more weight than the control babies, who were not offered this extra comforting. Dr. Salk believes the babies may have gained this weight because they used up less of their energy through crying.

It has been pointed out that mothers all over the world hold their babies in their left arms, whether or not they are right-handed or left-handed. Apparently this holding must be largely instinctive, since few mothers are aware that the baby is close to the sound of the maternal heartbeat. Yet one young mother sampling cosmetics in a department store while carrying her dormant four-month-old daughter in a canvas sling remarked to the saleslady, "Do you know my baby can actually feel my heart going? The rhythm puts her to sleep, and that's why she can sleep through all of this!"

When he is about four months old, a baby may recognize his father's footsteps and react happily, or he will react with all of his muscles to a music box, or to a record that he has come to know. There are some babies who may hum or make crooning sounds to music earlier than this. And they are not likely to be musical geniuses in the making, either! Mother's voice, as we know, is usually selected from all other voices as pretty special in the earliest months. One mother often sang a particular song to her baby during his first four months. His grandmother tried to sing the same song, but was somewhat miffed to discover that while he tolerated her voice, as soon as his own mother (no vocalist, to be sure) took over the tune he became enraptured. Just as with every other kind of response, the response to sound varies from baby to baby. Some mothers report that after they have sung the same lullabye or favorite melody to their babies just a few times, the babies begin to expect this song, and gradually it takes on meaning: it is lights-out now and time to go to sleep. (Note that this may mean a peaceful night for all.)

When the baby tries to communicate in other ways than by crying, you will know he has reached a new landmark in his development. It means he knows he can evoke a response from those around him when he feels *good,* too. Crying, as he has found out, is not the only way. Perhaps he feels that by making babbling sounds he can make some social conquests. He babbles, and others reply.

Your delight and approval of his efforts "conditions" him in a way to make even further efforts and sets him on the road to the future, when he will want to put language to the use of expressing his thoughts and needs and feelings. A baby is very sensitive to the intonation of his parents' voices and gets to know soon when they approve or disapprove of him.

Many mothers and fathers cannot help but talk baby talk to their babies, and sometimes feel self-conscious and silly if anyone happens to be around. Others, fortunately, are not so inhibited, nor have they been influenced by stern traditions that admonish, "If you use baby talk with your infant, he will fail to speak distinctly and properly later on." Baby talk does not retard speech development. (And few parents keep it up all the time.) In fact, your wish to be in communication with your baby—in whatever language appeals to you, be it gibberish or King's English—will produce in him the motivation he needs to respond verbally. Baby talk is a language of love, even used at times between lovers.

STIMULATING

This word has been used quite a bit up to now. What does it really mean?

In terms of Baby, stimulation includes all the things mentioned up to now, things that appeal to a baby's senses; to his

Soothing, Stimulating, and Spoiling

ears, eyes, skin, muscles, and mind. A baby who is left lying alone for long periods in his crib without toys or the human voice for distraction is on the short end of experiences that stimulate his senses. A baby may also receive unbearable amounts of stimulation when he is constantly fussed over, picked up, bounced and tickled, played with, poked at, and jounced about. Or he may be overstimulated if people are forever shaking rattles, mobiles, cradle-gyms, etc., at him. He may—as do adults—"want to get away from it all."

A fair share of stimulation helps the baby go out on his own to explore and experiment. He acquires much of his initiative through the successful contacts he has had with you—or another equally loving caregiver or givers—and begins to associate people with pleasure and satisfaction. When he is between four and six months, roughly speaking, he may enjoy active play with you. He may grasp your finger and try to pull himself up to a sitting position, or he may laugh with you, roll over, and wriggle from one corner of the crib or playpen to another.

According to Dr. David E. Schecter, Associate Clinical Professor, Department of Psychiatry, Albert Einstein College of Medicine, who has made careful studies of babies under one year of age, "mutual playfulness is a model of freedom and spontaneity in human relatedness." He feels this mutual play between the baby and those around him prepares him for later "communication, language and social collaboration, as well as a means of overcoming destructiveness." However, as Dr. Schecter also points out, if a baby is overstimulated, he becomes distressed and will end the play.

With all of this stimulating and playing, the baby also needs to have periods when he can play quietly in his crib or playpen with an object or two, or lie on his back and maybe kick or pull at some dangling toy. He does not need someone in the room all the time.

Being able to remain alone at times and not feel lonely is a great achievement, an asset for living itself. This capacity has its origins in early infancy, and starts out through the experience of "being alone, as an infant and small child, in the presence of mother," as Dr. D. W. Winnicott once wrote. Although mother and child may not be exchanging words, the baby knows his mother is "there" emotionally as well as physically—even if she isn't constantly in the room. Mother may be quietly reading or attending to other matters, but each knows that the presence of the other person is important to both. Baby has an inner feeling that his mother would respond if he needed her.

SPOILING

By now, some parents may begin to look at each other and ask, "Isn't all this attention going to *spoil* our baby?" Others might go even further and remark, "*He's* not going to run *our* lives!" or "We're just not going to cater to his whims," or "A baby has to learn to rely on himself," or "We don't want a spoiled brat in our home!"

All such anxious concerns make a lot of sense. But the truth of the matter is that a baby under the age of four or five months or so has not yet acquired the necessary mental equipment to figure out how to run the lives of others; his "whims" (wants) are still his needs; he cannot yet rely on himself; picking up the baby when he needs solace or some response has nothing to do with *spoiling*. Certainly—and it has been said before—if the baby is overstimulated and over-attended to, he loses the freedom with which to develop his own perceptive abilities and ways through which he can make his needs known.

To further clarify the issue of spoiling, we need to take a good look at what frustration is all about.

One of the most endearing and lovable traits in a human being is his capacity to be patient, to wait a while until some need or wish can be satisfied. This kind of person doesn't get angry when he can't always have what he wants when he wants it. He is pleasant to have around and is usually a fairly contented human being. More than this, he is likely to be effective and productive, for the capacity to endure a reasonable amount of frustration is basic for the ability to concentrate, to figure things out, and to solve problems.

Soothing, Stimulating, and Spoiling

This capacity to sustain some frustration and tension does not spring up suddenly out of the blue in childhood or adulthood. Rather, it develops slowly, gradually, imperceptibly—starting as early as the first months, weeks, even days of a baby's life. And, paradoxical as it may seem, it develops best in those children whose earliest needs are usually met, as shown in the Johns Hopkins study described in Chapter 3. The baby who is *not* frustrated often is taught to *endure* frustration, and the converse is also true. The baby who is often frustrated becomes more and more demanding, because, among other things, he is never sure that he is getting, or going to get, all that should be coming to him. He is always on guard.

This does not mean to imply you can never fail your baby, or that you must knock yourself out all the time to satisfy him. You are not failing your baby if you are not with it every minute. To repeat, some frustration in a baby's life is inevitable—even necessary—if he is to move forward in his development and learn how to cope.

As any parent already must have discovered, no matter how conscientious she is, no matter how devoted she is in tending to her baby's needs, her baby is *going* to be frustrated at times. It cannot be helped, because there are other realities to contend with. There are other members of the family, the food on the stove, the phone, the doorbell, a mother's own personal needs, and much else. Yet it is important that the baby's satisfactions outweigh his disappointments. These frustrations, however, need to come in small but tolerable doses if they are to be overcome. At a tender age, a baby can become so overpowered by frustration that he may abandon all natural attempts to cope with it and master it. He either may fight helplessly and ineffectively through constant whining and crying, or he may just withdraw into himself. (In extreme cases a baby may keep on rocking and rocking in his crib or bang his head against it, or seek compensation through continuous genital self-stimulation or through other erotic body pleasures such as constant thumb-sucking.)

In the seven-year study conducted by Drs. Brody and Axelrad,

The Roots of Love

it was shown that those babies who had had repeated experiences of frustration, particularly at feeding times when their mothers paid no attention to their cues (experiences that often mirrored the mothers' attitudes and handling of their babies in other ways), found it very difficult to concentrate when tested at the end of their first year of life. The researchers observed that these babies handled the objects put before them in a perfunctory way, or with impatience. In some cases, they pushed the objects away and at moments gave other evidence of real anxiety.

At the same time, there is no reason to believe that the baby who sets up a racket and howls for his food when hungry is an impatient baby who is not learning how to put up with some waiting and frustration. He may have learned, rather, to firmly ask for what he needs. And it takes a long time for many a baby to get the message that he *will* be satisfied eventually.

One of the babies in the study was a good example of how a tense, irritable, and nervous infant can change by being "understood."

At six weeks of age, Teddy could not seem to relax. "He is a bundle of nerves," his mother explained. "He kicks and squirms and stiffens up and yells at the slightest noise." He often became so tense and rigid that it was a trial to dress and undress him. However, Teddy was fed, handled, and talked to with such sympathetic understanding that by the time he was a year old it was hard to believe he was the same baby. He was cheerful, interested in people and in toys, and showed a high level of interest and curiosity during the testing period. Teddy stood up well under the tension that invariably accumulates during testing. What had happened to induce this change in him?

Dr. Brody reported that his mother (and father, too, since these parents were college graduate students who took turns looking after him) handled him with exceptional sensitivity to and awareness of his particular personality and responses. "When Teddy was picked up, he was talked to soothingly, but it wasn't overdone. He was often left by himself, but never when he was in distress. Gradually, a trust was built up in him that his waiting period would end shortly." Dr. Brody continued, "His

Soothing, Stimulating, and Spoiling

parents noticed that Teddy would become agitated when they burped him, so they tried instead to hold him, rather than pat him, until his bubble came up. 'Get busy, young man' his mother would murmur softly as she cajoled him to continue with his feeding. While his parents did not overwhelm him with solicitude, they adapted themselves to their infant's ways, yet also helped him to adapt to their expectations."

The progress of the 131 babies has been carefully followed up into their seventh year. The researchers have good evidence now to indicate that the intellectual and social development of the school beginners, including their adaptability to new situations and new people and their capacity to put up with frustration, reflects the patterns that were established between the mothers and babies during their first year.

To sum up: Through all the various happy experiences of his first six months or so of life, a baby becomes more adequately prepared to accept the necessary limitations on pleasure and activity that his mother and others must impose on his next stage of development. He finds it easier then to accept some delays, to postpone pleasures, and to invest his energies into learning how to master his environment. By the time he has reached the end of his first year, he will have come a long way in learning how to wait.

Frustration comes to all in life. The best way to strengthen a human being's capacity to meet it, is to meet his needs as much as possible (not neglecting your own, of course) during his earliest months.

By the sixth month or sooner, or even a bit later, some remarkable events will take place in the baby's emotional development. He will be able to distinguish his mother and father from all the other people in his environment. At that time he will be showing his special preference for one person—the beginnings of his expression of love.

THE BABY FROM SIX MONTHS TO A YEAR

 CHAPTER FIVE

The Birth of Love

Just when the baby appears to have become more predictable and fun to be with, a series of events may enter his life to completely upset the apple cart. Up to this point his eating and sleeping habits had become fairly regular. He had made friends with strangers as well as with relatives. He could entertain himself nicely; he didn't seem to be entirely dependent upon his mother in this way, and all told, life with Baby was shaping up well. But suddenly the baby's behavior may take an odd turn, which leaves his poor mother completely bewildered until she begins to understand what this new behavior means.

At some point, between the ages of six and nine months (or as early as five or as late as nine or ten), Baby feels he wants his mother (or mothering person) around him, near him, with him, practically all the time. The "others" will not do any more. And sometimes his wishes come on so strong that there is no risk of missing them. When Mother leaves him, even for a few minutes, he is apt to whimper or loudly protest, if not panic. He never acted this way before. He may show a distinct aversion to people whom he previously accepted and favored. In fact, this amiable socialite has now become a clinging vine.

What is this all about?

These quirks—actually the baby's way of expressing anxiety—happen to be connected with an enormous stride in his emotional development and in his ability to understand. He has just had his first experience with the feelings of love.

The Roots of Love

The baby is discovering for the first time that one person above all other persons has great emotional significance for him. And he is afraid of losing her.

The baby's very exclusive relationship with this one special person, steadily growing in these last months, has ripened to such an extent that he can clearly tell her apart from the others who figure in his life. Through his increasing capacity to remember—particularly his happy experiences—she has become for him the embodiment and memory of all past pleasures and joys, and the promise of those to come. The mother now seems to be the one who can best comfort him and fulfill his bodily and emotional needs. Her presence means as much to him as the food she brings him. The baby's feelings for her are becoming so strong that whether she pleases him or not, disappoints him and makes him angry, he still loves her. He touches her face, plays with her hair. When she feeds him, he in turn may try to feed her and put his cookie into her mouth.

As several psychologists have suggested, these responses are not too far removed from the responses of young lovers. They are part of the feelings that accompany the very first stirrings and yearnings of later love, and foreshadow some of the passion and ardor and feelings of exclusiveness in the love relationship ("You are the only one in the world for me!"). Naturally, these budding emotions are far removed from what we adults know as love. And the baby has a long, long way to go before he reaches the mature level of loving when he will be able to care for the happiness and well-being of the one he cherishes. Nevertheless, he has taken his initial step in that direction.

If these first shoots of love are tended to and carefully nourished, they will increase and multiply. This one special nurturer will not only have taught him how to love *her*, but how to love others. Father and siblings will be quickly included in that exclusive circle of favored ones, and then Grandma, Grandpa, the usual sitter, and others who previously may have been on his blacklist. And much later, the baby's capacity to love will have expanded to include those in the world outside of his family.

The Birth of Love

But first the baby has to go through more growing pains.

REACTIONS TO STRANGERS

Although, on the one hand, it is extremely flattering to be so singled out by your baby, you may find that his growing sense of "belonging" to you has some disadvantages. For a shorter or longer period, his "decision" * to sever former relationships may hamper your comings and goings. And, along with his discovery of his mother as very special and loved, of wanting her around, of shying away from familiar faces, he begins to show a tendency to shrink away from or shun *new* faces. The name of the game is "stranger reaction."

Now it is perfectly true that many babies go through this entire phase without much of a fuss. They accept the ever-widening circle of persons around them and merely show favoritism toward Mother and her presence. Some of these babies may have been quite used to a lot of traffic within the home, or have had much contact with a nurturing father, or have been frequently "included in" as visitors in the homes of family and friends. The reactions to strangers, which may range from some slight caution to anxiety, depend on whether the baby happens to be in home territory or away from home, whether the new person pounces upon him suddenly or gradually veers toward him. And, of course, much does depend upon how the baby happens to feel at the time; tired, ill or cranky, or bubbling with good health and spirits. Should the baby have been ill a good deal and have been handled frequently by nurses and doctors, it should come as no surprise to parents if he vaguely associates the newcomers with them.

Since babies are so unpredictable about strangers, you may find that your baby reacts in one of several ways:

A stranger or even a person with whom the baby is slightly acquainted enters the room. He (or she) may either approach the infant or keep his distance from him. The baby may be in Mother's arms or lap at the time, or he may be in his crib or

* Just a reminder again that a baby cannot yet make conscious "decisions."

The Roots of Love

playpen. Or he may be attempting to inch along the floor on his belly or on all fours. As the baby perceives the newcomer, he may look up and smile, then continue his activity, or he may just ignore him. He suddenly may be on guard and give the stranger a cool scrutiny, a "once-over," or he may watch the stranger carefully. Perhaps then he stops smiling and rudely begins to compare this face with what he has realized is his mother's face. Finding this other face wanting, he ceases to play and pulls back, or his body and face "freeze" in apprehension. He buries his head in Mother's shoulder or reaches up to her from where he is. Maybe in sheer terror he lets out a shriek.

To say the least, these latter reactions may cause you much embarrassment, and you are profuse in your apologies to your wounded friend or to poor Aunt Sarah, who has come all this way to meet Baby.

Apparently, the strange, the unknown is, at this point in the baby's development, so closely linked with his love for his mother and with his fear of her disappearance that in some strange way the newcomer just poses an added threat to his safety. At times the baby will act as if his mother had already left him, although she is still present.

As you continue to be nonplussed, and smile and speak warmly to the stranger, you give the baby a feeling that this person is really O.K. You can always explain the awkward situation to the "intruder" so this man or woman does not feel personally rejected. (And some adults do feel rejected in spite of knowing the baby is far too young to have such a highly developed sense of discrimination!) One ten-month-old infant set up such a commotion at the appearance of an uncle that his mother, upset by her baby's unfriendly behavior, scolded him and said impatiently, "What's gotten into you? Smile and say 'ta-ta' to Uncle Joe!"—all the while pushing the child closer to this innocent yet seemingly menacing relative. The baby, of course, became hysterical instead of just hesitant.

Should the stranger, or whoever, hand the baby a toy and the baby refuse to accept it, the fact that *you* play with the object and offer it to the child may suggest to him that you have given your

The Birth of Love

sanction to both the giver and toy. Since the infant is at an age when he is likely to imitate you—your gestures, expressions, and moods—he is more apt to follow your lead here too. Often, given time, the baby's normal curiosity will supersede his fears. He may then eagerly, or maybe only cautiously, proceed to investigate the stranger further and show his goodwill. Nevertheless, every encounter with a new person may, for a while, repeat this pattern. By encouraging the baby gently but not pushing him, and so with all other new experiences, you not only may help to make the unfamiliar familiar to him but you may help to make it novel and exciting.

Yet even after these reactions to strangers seem to have subsided, they are likely to appear again and again in one way or another throughout the child's first three years—and even after. And later on in adulthood, aren't we sometimes terrified of entering a room full of strangers, or of meeting new people?

REACTIONS TO SEPARATION

Closely related to but slightly independent of these reactions to strangers is the baby's fear of being separated from his mother. At this point he seems to have acquired a dim awareness that his total survival depends upon his caregiver. Furthermore, can anything be more upsetting than to first find your love and then to face separation soon after? In somewhat the same way, the baby finds it hard to let his mother go. It must have been the under-three-year-olds who inspired those songs of longing: "Lover Come Back to Me," "The Indian Love Call," "Night and Day," "What'll I Do [when you are far away . . .]" and their modern equivalents that make so many adolescents go dreamy.

A series of minor and major separations from loved ones is part of everyone's life history. These separations start at birth, then follow with weaning, and then separation from Mother at the time of which we are speaking; later come the first steps away from her, and then nursery school or day care. And so it goes throughout childhood, adolescence, and adulthood. Besides these expected separations are the distressing ones that can occur in

The Roots of Love

adult life: the breaking up of a love affair, the partings at wartime, desertion, divorce, and the painful separations of death.

Some adults are able to meet these difficult trials with a startling degree of stability; others are completely shattered by them. The fact that some can come through tragedies with fortitude, however, does not make the tragic occurrences less painful to them. And the ability to withstand stresses and strains and pain has little to do with being a "strong" or "weak" person. This capacity, or lack, is no reflection, either, on one's character, but rather has to do with factors that are way beyond our conscious control. To a large degree, the human being who in infancy felt securely loved and emotionally supported is usually sustained deep within himself by this love, drawing upon its reserves to see him through such times of buffeting.

The very young child, under three years of age, can be helped—although only very gradually—to meet some of the inevitable separation challenges of the future.

First we must understand what separation means to a child under the age of one year.

Before about the eighth month in a baby's life, according to the Swiss psychologist, Dr. Jean Piaget—who has made detailed studies on the development of intelligence in children—when a toy or some object the infant has played with is moved out of his sight, the baby is not likely to try to locate it. This is because he presumably reasons that the object no longer exists. Gone is gone. He may also not understand when his mother goes that *she* still exists. However, at some point *after* his eighth month or so, he will make a search for that toy or object (which has been hidden from him behind a screen or under a pillow), provided he has witnessed the hiding of the object. He then will remove the obstacle and retrieve the object, which he now is beginning to realize has an existence of its own—even when not in view. By this time, he is able to remember a hidden article, but just for a very short period. At the same time in his development and in much the same way, the baby is beginning to remember his absent loved mother. He can bring her to mind for just a little while longer than he can remember the hidden toy, primarily

The Birth of Love

since real feelings are attached to her which help to call her back in his mind—momentarily. If she leaves the room, the infant may repeatedly stare at the door through which she left, crawl toward the door, or gaze at the chair upon which she sat. (However, as we will see later, it may not be until his third year that the baby can *keep* the image of his mother vivid and alive within himself to sustain himself more easily during her absence.)

Yet there are a number of ways in which a baby of this age can find some reassurance that when Mother (and, very shortly, Daddy) leaves, she *will* return. Dr. Peter Neubauer suggests that "The mother separates *with* the child, not *from* him." By this he means the mother helps the child learn to take leave of her, helps him to manage his daily separations with less fear and with more confidence and ease.

The following section will take up just the everyday, brief separations of mother and child, and indicate some ways in which parents can help to strengthen the child's ability to tolerate them.

BRIEF SEPARATIONS

Peek-a-Boo

In this simple game that parents play almost automatically with their babies along with pat-a-cake, they cover the baby's eyes with their hands and "hide." Then, as the parents remove their hands, they "reappear." Baby is inclined to copy this game. He covers *his* eyes and you disappear—so he believes. He uncovers his eyes, and there you are once more! The infant loves this game—and its variations—and often squeals with delight at the magic feat. As he gets you to repeat this little trick and imitates it over and over again (and he could keep it up endlessly), he gains some sense of mastery and control over the situation. *He* has made you go, and *he* has made you return! In addition, he is further helped to understand that somehow you exist even when he cannot see you. Fun in itself, the peek-a-boo game is also said to help the child's feeling that he is a separate person (I am me and you are you), and facilitates to some extent the actual partings of mother and child. Later in childhood, the hide-and-seek games, universally adored by youngsters, accomplish some of the same. As the children seek the "lost" person, perhaps originally (and symbolically) the mother figure, they enjoy the slight but still controllable sense of danger, along with the rewarding and safe feeling of having retrieved the lost one again.

Taking Leave of a Crying Baby
Partings are truly sweet sorrow for the Diaper Brigade—*especially* for them. But none of this means that the baby's first loud protest should prevent parents from taking leave of their infant. A young child needs to have practice in getting used to these routine partings. Through this practice he learns several things:

- Yes, Mother *does* go away, but she always comes back.
- He will not lose her love.
- He can survive in her absence for short periods at a time.

Small doses of separation handled with care prepare a baby to cope with and adapt to later, longer separations.

But how does one—or can one—leave a crying baby?

Wanting to avoid a scene, the mother of a baby girl aged nine months crept out of the house after her baby had fallen asleep, leaving her with a strange, although trustworthy, sitter. The baby happened to awaken in the middle of her nap, and upon seeing this unfamiliar face, let out a terrified scream. The baby's sobs remained unabated until her mother returned home shortly thereafter. For weeks following this experience, the infant would cling to her mother every time anyone entered the home, vigilantly watching her every move. And, associating sleep with the disappearance of her mother, the baby and parents had a rough go of it at bedtime. All of this could have been avoided had the mother first "introduced" her baby to the sitter, staying with the two until they had become acquainted, and then let the baby know she was going to go out for a little while.

In order to keep the infant's trust and faith in human nature alive through these comings and goings that are both inevitable

The Birth of Love

and necessary—and this trust is so very fragile at this age—it makes sense *not* to sneak out when his back is turned, so to speak. An infant needs to prepare himself for his mother's exit, thereby learning to work out his own methods of tolerating and coping with the situation.

Some babies are already familiar with and like the substitute person or persons who will stand in for Mother when she takes shore leave, and are not apt to kick up a big fuss (except maybe for that brief period when Mother is first recognized). But more often than not, other babies are likely to hang on desperately to their mother at the first moment they sense she is going to depart. (Partings are often easier for the second baby in the family, who has his older sibling for company and familiarity. Besides, he usually takes his cues from the older one, who may already have made his peace with brief separations.)

No one will deny that listening to your baby's anguished cries as you depart tears at your heartstrings. And these poignant farewells may continue on and off throughout the child's first three years of life—or more. But normally his cries do not always indicate anxiety. Often they are a baby's way of vocalizing his momentary regrets. A mother's first impulse may be to cancel her appointment and stay home with her baby instead of going out. Normal enough. But if she acts on this impulse, strange as it may seem—granting that the baby is not sick, and has made friends with the sitter—she only postpones the inevitable partings, and this makes the coping harder for the baby *and* herself.

A baby usually gets to know, whether he protests or not, that Mother is here for keeps if:

- While at home, the baby can stay near you as you go about your work. If he can crawl, he will enjoy playing at your feet and pulling himself up on your knees.
- He can get a good amount of physical contact and snuggling, as he received when younger. Paradoxical as it seems, the holding may stimulate the clinger's urge to push away from you.
- Words are spoken that he may not understand but which imply that Mother is going out but will return.

The Roots of Love

- The key persons—outside of Father or a close relative—are one or two warm and genuinely interested motherly women or young girls whom you can call upon regularly.
- Before making an exit, you let the baby become well acquainted with the substitute, seeing to it that the substitute is well alerted about his fears. If she is willing to comfort him and play with him while you are gone, he may enjoy her "visits" the following times. (Sometimes, the baby will accept the stand-in and cling to her bodily, but as soon as he raises his head and sees she isn't you, he may howl.)

Once you have departed, your mind should be at rest if the sitter reports the baby's tears subsided soon after your departure. While these tears are *not* crocodile tears, because they are an initial reaction to a real event, he may *sound* more upset than he really is. This being so, if the tears soon stop, you should be encouraged to know that he is beginning to take hold of the problem and is becoming more comfortable with it.

Should the sitter tell you that the baby continued to wail after you left, or that he seemed completely disinterested in his toys or in exploring his little world, it might mean that the substitute is not really substituting for you, and you may need a substitute for *her!* Or it might mean that, for some unknown reason, the baby truly needs more of you at this point.

Should the baby continue to fuss in your absence, it might help matters to take him along with you—as much as you can—when you go out, at least for a while longer. The extra and possibly much-needed gift of reassurance of your continued love is likely to pay off, even if it does seem somewhat wearing for the time being.

If weaning or any other new adjustment is on the agenda, the temporary postponement of these changes will give the baby a chance to overcome his first separation reactions. Babies are better able to handle just one major adjustment at a time.

THE WORKING MOTHER

When a mother is fairly contented and happy, her baby is apt to reflect her well-being (barring his episodes of colic or illness). If

The Birth of Love

she longs instead to return to her job or occupation, or is bored or restless, finding herself jittery and chafing at the bit, naturally she will resent being cooped up with her infant. And to make matters worse, she may feel uncomfortably guilty for giving houseroom to such thoughts. There is little joy for a mother *or* baby if the mother is there just in body but not in spirit. These feelings are usually communicated to him nonverbally anyhow, and he may become confused as he senses her mixed messages.

Everyone will agree that if a mother who wants to, or needs to, work is able to find a part-time job while her baby is this young, or if she can manage to spend a couple of anxiety-free hours at home with her baby in between her work schedule, she and her child are fortunate. But it may also mean some pretty fancy footwork on her part. For the mother who works full-time, it is best for her and her baby if she postpones, if at all possible, returning to her job or full-time career until some time *after* the baby has singled her out as *the one* in his life. Once these bonds have become established and firm, it may be easier for the baby to gradually share his newly developed capacity for love and affection with some other mothering person. (When a mother goes to work prior to the time when the baby comes to know and prefer her, then the infant may develop his first emotional attachment to her stand-in. But more about this later.)

Of course, if you are able to find one (working full- or part-time), the person best able to help you swing this operation is a steady, motherly woman who knows the needs of babies and who enjoys caring for them. Then consider yourself blessed. Changes in substitutes—as has been said before—are very hard on a baby, since he needs continuity in his relationships. The disappearance of a loved mother surrogate can cause him to grieve as much as he'd grieve were his mother to forsake him. That is, unless his mother can take time off from work to replace his loss. (And, as we shall see later, babies from this age on can mourn in much the same way as do adults, with the same symptoms: loss of sleep, no appetite, listlessness, refusal to be consoled, etc.) In addition, a rapid succession of sitters, nurses, or housekeepers, to each of whom a baby becomes attached, may

The Roots of Love

impair the development of his capacity to love. Such ruptures in relationships, such bereavements, can force the child to defend himself against future hurt and desertions by closing up inside himself and blocking off all deep feeling. Not wanting to risk closeness to anyone for fear of feeling pain again, such a child, as an adult, may decide to "play it cool." Inevitably, this means leading a safe but emotionally flat and empty life. (Babies in institutions will run to anyone who pays attention to them, but this is because they belong to no one. Since they have not been able to grow roots of love, the institution babies may, like the "cool" adult, find any one person interchangeable with another.)

Now, of course, the picture isn't all that gloomy. From a practical point of view, it is quite difficult today to find a steady housekeeper or sitter. *But where Mother (and/or Father) remains actively and lovingly in the foreground during a series of substitute changes, the impact of these losses may be diluted.* Somehow the baby comes to realize that his mother has been and will be there all along, behind these other relationships. She is his mother and nothing can change this.

The working mother faces another conflict. Sharing her baby's love with another woman who has come to take her place during the day is never easy. The fact that part of her baby's love roots have been grown into this substitute (nurse, grandmother, housekeeper, or whoever) is hard to take. And hearing her baby cry when this pseudomother departs for her time off or goes home can truly cut deep. It is only natural that pangs of jealousy may interfere temporarily with a mother's appreciation for everything the stand-in is doing for her child.

If you happen to be in this dilemma, be reassured in knowing you are doing the very best that is possible for your baby's emotional health and well-being just by providing this warm person to whom the baby *can* become attached. You—and he—will discover soon enough that *you* are really the important figure in his life. And, as he gets to be a little older, your constant affection and empathy, your very special relationship with him, will be making lasting impressions on his love life. These roots then will be transplanted back to you.

The Birth of Love
HAPPINESS IS A CUDDLY SOMETHING

Most babies seem to devise and invent ingenious ways of meeting life's pressures and growing pains. One of these means is through the discovery of a "do-it-yourself" comforting agent in the guise of a blanket, diaper, scarf, piece of cloth, or soft furry animal toy, which the baby clutches, caresses, cuddles, and/or sucks.

Many are familiar with Linus and his famous "security blanket" in the comic strip "Peanuts." Linus has an almost universal appeal because he rings a bell in many of us, touching off memories of our own lost comforter of long ago. Many of us had to have this object next to us at bedtime, and we often dragged it along (to our parents' dismay) on visits, during times of fatigue, stress, or illness. And woe if that blanket or "cuddly" was temporarily mislaid or—even worse yet—lost. The entire family would be enlisted in a frenzied search for it, and *no* substitute would do here.

These "transitional objects," as Dr. D. W. Winnicott has named them, are in a way transitional, since they are things, not part of the baby, yet not as separate as the toys he will play with later on.

A baby may first take to such an article around nine or ten months or so—earlier or much later. As he presses it close to his face and nose, he finds its warmth and its familiar smell comforting. While it most certainly may not look so, the use of these objects indicates a step forward in the infant's development. It shows he has been able to form a relationship to something that is not as close as his mother or thumb (although some babies may suck on their thumbs as well while clutching the object). Baby's first soft possession does remind him somehow of Mother, particularly when he has to break away from her as he is put into his crib and when she is absent. It also helps him to withdraw from his active life in the outside world and drift off to sleep.

Bedtime and naptime can be particularly threatening moments for the child who is going through his first wave of separation fears. Meanwhile, as he nears the end of his first year, he is beginning to work out some means of overcoming little anxieties and to tolerate minor frustrations. Along with his parents' gentle but firm reassurance before nap and bedtime, and with their giving of a little extra holding, patting, and soothing, the cuddly—for which they can be grateful—may now help him to bridge his growing sense of separateness and aloneness.

Anna Freud in *Normality and Pathology in Childhood* points to another aspect of the transitional object's importance as

> . . . a permanently controlled possession, in contrast to the mother, who is not under the child's control and whose independent coming and going, appearance and disappearance, threaten the child with feelings of insecurity and separation distress.

When the child is somewhat older, and feels angry, he may dash the cuddly object to the ground, fling it across a room, drag it, treat it miserably. But soon, in remorse or in a better mood, he takes it back into his favor, caresses it tenderly once again, and hangs onto it for dear life. And, unlike a real person, the object cannot retaliate!

In later childhood, the song may be ended but the melody lingers on, and we see the ten- or eleven-year-old girl who is beginning to sprout tiny breasts lying sound asleep in her bed clutching her teddy bear. And in adulthood, maybe these early cuddlys become goosedown quilts and pillows, soft beds, sweaters, woolly and furry coats that caress and protect us—all pleasant but distant substitutes for the long-relinquished enveloping warmth of Mother.

EMOTIONAL ASPECTS OF WEANING

Weaning from the Breast

Few babies go directly from breast to cup. Perhaps when the baby has been breast-fed through his first year (or a little less) and has had supplementary bottles as well as solids and cup feedings, he may show his willingness to forego sucking entirely. However, other babies weaned this late still want a bottle, especially when they are very hungry, or at nighttime when tired. Most babies are weaned earlier, from breast to bottle.

The Birth of Love

Breast-weaning implies another shift in the mother-child relationship. It is a baby's first important step away from his intimate body relationship with Mother to a more "independent" way of life. He may be better prepared for this change at the six- or seven-month stage, when he has indicated his growing interest in *things* more than *persons*. Nevertheless, at whatever stage he is weaned, the whole process is made easier for the baby when his mother continues to hold and cuddle him while giving him the bottle.

If weaning is abrupt and accompanied by an actual separation from his mother, the interruption can upset the baby. A word of caution about two other related factors: Should the child be in the midst of intense stranger or separation reactions, it may be wise not to begin the breast-weaning at that very time. If the baby is in the midst of other stresses which he cannot help but "feel"—an illness in the family, a death, a move from one home to another—it is best to avoid burdening him at the same time with adjusting to another change in his life.

As for a mother's feelings, many mothers who have successfully and joyfully breast-fed their babies find that weaning is somewhat of an emotional wrench. All along, this experience has been such a gratifying and "gutsy" one that it also means an adjustment for *her*. Some mothers undergo a sense of loss. (A number of doctors attribute some of this feeling to changes in body chemistry that take place as the body shifts to the prenursing state once more.) Others feel as if they had been deprived of a basic function in providing for their infants. Even mothers who have bottle-fed their babies sometimes feel the rift of the close body tie with their infants. One mother said wistfully, "I feel as if Betty (all of six months) doesn't need me any more!" (The need for Mother will continue from this point in time on through adolescence, but at each new phase, we parents need to shift gears in order to adapt to the new and different ways in which our children will be needing us.)

Ultimately, as the baby is weaned, there are many compensations. A mother may be relieved to find herself freer to enjoy things or take a nap without needing to keep an eye on the clock

The Roots of Love

to remind her she must interrupt whatever she is doing to feed her baby—now, she can let someone else take over.

Weaning from the Bottle

When is an infant ready for this step? There are no hard and fast rules here either. Readiness seems to depend in part upon the individual baby and the strength of his sucking drives, and on his own mother's feelings about weaning. Watchwords like "easy does it" and "gradually" are the best guides. Here, too—as with breast-weaning—an *abrupt* interruption of sucking can be a shock to the baby, equivalent to a major catastrophe in an adult's life! In one way or another, he may then, in childhood and adulthood, continue to search for some replacement (usually a poor substitute) for those oral pleasures he had to give up or lose so suddenly in infancy.

Many will agree that those who have thoroughly enjoyed a certain pleasure or privilege can more easily relinquish it when necessary than those who have only partly enjoyed the pleasure —and who still want their fill. It stands to reason that if you haven't had enough of something you like, you continue to go after it.

As for other signs of the baby's readiness, he often gives those clues during feedings. At that time he may become more readily distracted, smile at others, let go of the nipple, move about a lot, and altogether show his fascination in the things that are around him—all of which signal that he may be ready to move ahead. (The doctor no doubt will have given you his suggestions as to how and when to introduce liquids from a cup and solids.) It is apt to take several more months of bottle along with milk in a cup before a baby is ready to take all of his milk this way.

Should the baby angrily shove the cup away, he is saying in no uncertain terms that he couldn't care less about the whole idea at present.

One can always offer to help a child move toward growing up by recognizing his readiness, but *he* has to follow up from there on. One cannot force a child. He has his own inner electronic

The Birth of Love

clock. Provided his environment is adequate, he usually picks up the cues in his own good time.

In each stage of his development or "unfolding," even through adolescence, the child will be relinquishing some childish pleasures to reach—and also delight in reaching—a higher level of maturity and experience. But as he takes his giant steps forward, it is to be expected he will also take some chicken steps backward from time to time. And there never are any clear boundaries from one stage of growth and development to the next. There is bound to be much overlapping and backtracking.

SEPARATING FROM MOTHER— ON HIS OWN

As the baby ends his first year (approximately) he has acquired powers of locomotion, and he creeps, crawls, inches along on his belly, or stands up and navigates by holding onto one chair and moving to the next. Other babies can even totter about on their own. But regardless, they do get around. Some babies can even say a few words. And Mother has to be nimble and quick while diapering him, since his urge is so strong to climb, pull himself up, and turn around. Some mothers try to distract the baby by giving him a toy he can hold onto, or they just give up and learn to diaper him backward, or even while he stands.

The former lap baby has now begun to separate from his mother on his own steam. It is a kind of psychic separation which *he* initiates. Dr. Margaret S. Mahler, Clinical Professor of Psychiatry, Albert Einstein College of Medicine, and Director of Research at the Masters' Children's Center in New York City, describes this psychic separation process as "separation-individuation." Prior to this phase, when he was around five or six months, the baby had just begun his "hatching" out—as Dr. Mahler refers to it—from his feelings of being one with his mother. During the separation-individuation phases, the baby gradually begins to find his individuality, to become a relatively independent little person (from a geographic point of view, that is!) by the age of three.

The Roots of Love

Looking back, it was nice in some ways to have had a completely dependent little baby to care for. Many a mother's arms ache after her child has "decided" to leave them. But you are not out of a job yet. It will be quite some time before little Sam or Mary goes off to college! In the meantime, you can pause a bit and see your baby from a different perspective. From a distance, you can better watch him as he proudly accomplishes new feats. And now you have more time to relish the baby who may even seem a sort of companion. As mothers will often say, "He's getting to be a real little person now!"

At the same time, the child experiences his separateness—his "me-ness"—*in the presence of his mother or her stand-in.* With her nearby, he knows that as he moves a tiny bit away from her, he can still return to her for a hug, for snuggling, albeit the emotional and physical contact doesn't last too long and he pushes away from her soon again. But during these toddler years, each push further away from his mother arouses new fears and anxious moments. When these occur, he makes a beeline for her, since Mother is "home base" in Dr. Mahler's words. Needless to say, he may wish to be a tiny baby once more when he is under stress or ill, and want to be soothed and fussed over. This is a tendency also shared by many of us adults who often behave somewhat like cranky children when we are upset or tired or ill.

In our long struggles to find our identities and achieve independence, we continue to pull away and separate from our protectors. Yet throughout life we also have a tendency to pull back. Most of our adult life is a battle between two opposing drives: for independence and dependence; for closeness and separateness; for individuation and for union with another human being. We overcome our separateness again in sexual union when we experience what one psychiatrist has called "a temporary relinquishing of the separating boundaries . . ." But then we soon become aware again of our individual selves. No one ever achieves absolute independence. We are all dependent on one another: interdependent. In terms of emotional health, total self-sufficiency is as suspect as the parasitic clinging of the overly dependent. Yet even in our most independent states we

The Birth of Love

are, as with the young child, supported by knowing that when in need there is always someone to turn to, someone we trust. For the mature adult, that someone may even be far away. This knowledge held within us that we can be soothed, reassured, and bolstered emotionally at times, helps to reinforce us against the many pressures of life.

The baby should now be facing life with trust and with happy expectations. With all of his "exploratory forays," he will derive a sense of his competence—and also fallibility (and, one could well add, his "*fall*ability"!). While at times he impresses himself and us by his exploits, he will meet physical hazards as well as many "No's!" from his parents. He will feel and act quite angry with you at times and experience his first slight twinges of guilt and fear that his anger expressed—or even unexpressed—will endanger your love for him. During this next year and more, the child will be testing your love and patience. But he will come to know even as you make your demands known and understood, that your love and acceptance of him remain steadfast.

THE ONE- TO TWO-YEAR-OLD

CHAPTER SIX

The Toddler's Love Affair with the World

THE YOUNG EXPLORER

The toddler's "love affair with the world"—words coined by Dr. Phyllis Greenacre, noted psychiatrist and psychoanalyst—best describes the pint-sized explorer's exuberance and elation over his new discovery: the universe.

From the time he becomes a "junior toddler," as Dr. Margaret Mahler prefers to call him (roughly from about ten or twelve months to eighteen months), and then enters into and finishes his "senior" toddlerhood (from about eighteen months to twenty-four months), he investigates with gusto anything and everything within reach—and beyond his reach. He is constantly behind, under, over, into, and onto. He seems almost punchdrunk over his new-found powers to push and pull and navigate, and his mother can become dizzy just trying to keep an eye on him. In his first attempts to use the upright position, he may teeter and totter, then, sometimes impatient with such efforts that slow him down in his explorations, he may decide he can make it faster by going back to a rapid crawl.

The toddler's day, even that of a conservative and cautious toddler, is just one endless treasure hunt, and his treasure troves may be the lower bookshelf, the magazine rack, the contents of the wastebasket or garbage pail, the kitchen cupboards, and of course the clothes closet. The back sides of sofas and armchairs, as he peers over them, have a special fascination, as do tabletops.

The Roots of Love

During mealtimes he may turn the filled cup of milk upside down just to find out what the bottom looks like. And, enthusiastically grabbing the spoon from his mother in attempts to feed himself, he may smear his face, hair, clothes, and the floor with applesauce.

As part of his testing, experimenting, and following of impulses—not aware yet that there are such things as limits, but which he will discover all too soon—he may happily tweak the cat's tail or sink his teeth into Mommy's or Daddy's neck in innocent (?) delight.

Is the junior toddler made of rubber, one wonders as he continuously tumbles down without injuring himself or minding the bumps, or do those diapers stem his falls?

With all his preoccupations and high-riding, the junior toddler—hardly more than a baby in many ways—still wants to play it safe as far as his love life is concerned. Although he may not *seem* to notice whether his mother is close by or not, he periodically checks up on her to make sure she *is* there. He may then reach out to her to be picked up and held and snuggled; to receive what Dr. Mahler and her associates have termed "emotional refueling." Then, contented and reassured by his mother's hugs, he pushes off her lap to ride away again. The junior toddler wants and needs to feel his separateness from Mother. Yet, should she rebuff him or try to push him away when he is in need of her presence—perhaps believing it is time for him to learn how to "stand on his own feet"—her efforts are likely to rebound. As Dr. John Bowlby, a renowned British psychoanalyst and child psychiatrist who has made extensive studies of the effects of separation on the young child, explains it, the results are apt to be "the opposite of what is intended—he becomes more clinging than ever."

Later, when the toddler reaches about the second half of his second year (senior toddlerhood), he may become more acutely aware of his physical separateness from his mother. He may suddenly realize how utterly helpless and vulnerable he actually is. Now, when he hurts himself, he is somewhat surprised, even shocked and disillusioned—seeming to have lost some of that

The Toddler's Love Affair with the World

blind faith in himself so obvious a few months back. Did he overestimate his powers? ("How can this happen to *me?*") In addition to this letdown feeling, he also has to come to terms with the fact that Mother and Father and the others are not always *right on the spot* to rescue him from his daring maneuvers. But as he reaches to them for solace, their soothing and sympathetic assurances, rather than "Be a big boy (or girl) now and don't cry," helps him to renew his courage and continue to feel his oats.

During this year or so, particularly around the eighteen-month stage, the toddler often goes through new waves of separation anxieties (and more about this soon). This means, however, that his mother not only has to chase him all over the place to keep him out of peril's way, but also has the renewed separation problem to deal with. And to boot, the toddler seems to be more demanding than he was several months ago. His demands, however, are on a rather different level. He wants to share with Mother his every new experience, his every new accomplishment. He brings to her the toys and objects he loves the best and fondly dumps them onto her lap. Her admiration is his sweetest reward.

All of which is just one more step in the growth of his capacity to love. He is learning to share the spoils of life with a loved person; he wants to have her enjoy with him the goodness of life. And how marvelous it is to share pleasures with the beloved! How deeply satisfying it is for us to receive admiration from the one we love the most.

In the toddler's first attempts to find an identity, a "me," as mentioned several times before, he will try to venture away from his mother. And she will want to gently encourage his steps away from her. If he is *sure* she is standing by in the wings to prompt him when he needs her, his basic trust in her and in himself will expand. To his mother's dismay again, he may need and decide to cling to her desperately at the most awkward moments: when she is in a mad rush to get things done, is on the telephone, has to open the stove door or go to the toilet. Although he is ready now to accept little frustrations and postponements, sometimes there is a quality to his clinging and tugging that tells you he is undergoing a fair amount of anxiety that needs relief. Shifting

The Roots of Love

priorities in his favor at such moments—at least when they *can* be shifted—not only helps him to overcome the unknown reasons for his anxiety now, but it pays off later. The more his anxieties diminish through your succor, the more his self-confidence strengthens. This being so, he learns to become *less* dependent upon you. And the more autonomy he acquires, the freer you will be from his demands.

One of the toddler's earliest triumphs are those first steps he takes as he learns to walk.

The Swedish philosopher, Sören Kierkegaard, gives the "feel" of the child's ambivalence and a sensitive mother's response to him in the following passage from his book *Purity of Heart*, written in 1846. The child is taking his first steps:

> She is far enough away from him so that she cannot actually support him, but she holds out her arms to him. She imitates his movements, and if he totters, she swiftly bends as if to seize him, so that the child might believe he is not walking alone. The truly loving mother can do no more if she really intends for the child to walk alone. And yet, she does more. Her face beckons like a reward, an encouragement. Thus, the child walks alone with his eyes fixed on his mother's face not on the difficulties in his way. He supports himself by the arms that do not hold him and constantly strives towards the refuge in his mother's embrace, little suspecting that in the very same moment that he is emphasizing his need of her, he is proving that he can do without her because he is walking alone.*

Although it is the mother who is leading the child in the above passage, it stands to reason that an equally understanding and empathic father could substitute for her.

Father becomes more important than ever now that his child-baby has reached junior and senior toddlerhood. He is of tremendous help to his young child as the toddler tries to pull himself away from his still close physical tie to his mother. Father offers a rather different kind of stimulation. Perhaps he rough-

---

* Dr. E. James Anthony has used this excerpt in a chapter in the book *Separation-Individuation, Essays in Honor of Margaret S. Mahler*, edited by John B. McDevitt and Calvin F. Settlage, International Universities Press, New York, 1971.

The Toddler's Love Affair with the World

houses a bit, swinging his child into the air, giving him piggy-back rides, romping and playing with him in general. There is even a difference in the way he lifts his child. Besides, the toddler enjoys the novelty of spending time with someone (unlike Mother) with whom he is not so emotionally involved. Both child and mother find relief when this other duo have their fling together. And, at this time in the toddler's life, Father has not yet become a person who represents restraint and conflict—although his turn is soon to come.

TRIALS AND TRIBULATIONS OF MOTHER AND TODDLER

Some find the toddler around the halfway mark between one and two years of age a delight. They see the child as "cute," "fun," "interesting to watch," and prefer this stage to infancy. For others, the phase is a mixed bag, with alternating currents of delight and despair running throughout each day. In part, this is because there are times when a mother and her toddler's needs mesh, and times when they are diverse.

By and large, however, child and parent have slightly different objectives and goals. The toddler does not want to be crossed or stopped in his fascinating activities, feats of daring, and conquest of space on account of "danger," "character development," or parental worries about his future. It is the moment, the NOW, that counts for him. (By the time he is nineteen or so, he should have outgrown this point of view!)

Parents of course are on another wave length. They rightfully cannot always let him do what he wants to do. You *are* interested in the future, in the child's character development, in protecting him from danger, in protecting your property, and in preserving your own sanity! You are faced with the delicate task of distinguishing between the toddler's needs and wants—not necessarily the same any more. With it all, you are trying to strike a reasonable balance between encouraging the child's strivings for autonomy, keeping alive his delicious curiosity and zest for life—yet limiting him for his sake and for your own. It all

The Roots of Love

adds up to walking a tightrope. Small wonder, then, if you look back with nostalgia to the days when you could quietly sit reading a book while the baby was sleeping or playing safely in his crib, carriage, or playpen. Or, you may be looking ahead to the day when your busy wanderer will be ready to enter a play group, nursery school, or a good day-care center.

The writer, Anne Richardson Roiphe, a mother of five, once again captures the essence of the feelings of many mothers as they grapple with the conflicts of these days. She writes in *Vogue*:

> Initially, I thought it was dear, sweet to see her assert herself, refuse to eat the food I had prepared, rush out the playground gate; flush her socks down the toilet; but as the weeks went by, I began to see that something important had forever ended. The time when I had nursed her happily and we fell asleep together and it was hard for me to think of myself as someone single, separate—that innocent Eden was over. Now, with the books pulled out of the bookcase, my child and I glared at each other. Separate, opponents, two people at odds and alone. Temporarily, the terror of aloneness might drive the child back onto my lap; we'd listen to music together, turn the pages of a book together, and reunite for a while till the struggle would begin again. She was not a part of me, not controlled by me, nor I a part of her or controlled by her; and that was difficult for us both.

Clearly, the toddler, either junior or senior, who has his own strong and primitive wishes has to go through the difficult trials now of learning how to adapt himself to the wishes of those closest to him, those whose love he cherishes and desperately needs. He is making the discovery that his Garden of Eden has gates. The gatekeepers shut him out now when he doesn't follow certain rules that often he isn't yet able to comprehend. The guardians of his garden do not laugh or smile or play with him when he has done something they don't like. And their voices sound terrible. They surely are not much fun to be with at those moments.

At this point in his life, he is just becoming aware of one sad lesson about love. Love does not come *absolutely* free any more. It seems as if he will have to earn this precious reward and give up

The Toddler's Love Affair with the World

things he wants to do in order to receive it. He is just beginning to perceive too that he will have to give as well as get.

"NO!"

At some time during the second year, the baby usually begins to talk. Some acquire the skill early, and some later, while others suddenly burst forth in short sentences after a long silence that worried the whole family, and they stun their listeners with the extent of their vocabulary. But the child's speech development does help in giving you an inkling of what it is your child needs, wants, or fears. And it gives *him* an important tool now with which to further the mastering of his environment.

Of all the words that have meaning to the toddler, the word "No!" tops the list. To us, the word signifies a rebuff, a negation, a finality—at least when expressed by an adult. Yet when a toddler comes out with it, more often than not he isn't at all sure, nor even expects, he will be taken seriously. And it does seem unfair that his "No!" should come under the category—at least to some—of "negative behavior." Actually, his "no" is the toddler's *positive* way of asserting himself as an individual, of declaring that he is on the map and has rights. If little Mary is in "that mood" and has said "no" to a number of requests, and you ask her if she wants some ice cream or a lollipop or whatever she loves best, her emphatic and automatic "No!" that may follow should give you some idea of her value judgments at this moment.

When you consider the terrific amount of courage this miniature David displays as he looks up to his giant parent Goliath and figuratively slays him with his bland "No!" (and you *do* appear as a giant from where he stands), you may be amazed or amused, if not altogether enchanted.

Leontine Young, for many years Director of the Newark Child Service Association in New Jersey, and author of several books, graphically describes the situation. "The general idea runs something like this. 'I may be small and I may be weak, but I'm a person and just because you're big, don't get the idea you can

The Roots of Love

push me around.' The ubiquitous 'no' is a defense system always on alert with a definite tendency to regard all bystanders, particularly bigger ones, as potential encroachers on the new citadel." Dr. Young goes on to say that this continuous "no" has an effect on parents somewhat like the Chinese water torture that just monotonously drips away on parental patience, "that can upon occasion bring the most solid parent to the screaming point."

Yet, as with the young adolescent many years later, who says night when you say day (and the nearly two-year-old resembles him in more ways than one, especially in his need to lift off and try out his wings), if you can maintain some balance and humor, you are likely to get through this stage in one piece.

The seeming guerrilla warfare that goes on sometimes between you and your child need not develop into an open pitched battle. Rather than confront the toddler and make an issue of tiny matters—besides making things more difficult for yourself—it is usually possible to get around most any situation *before* it becomes an issue. (A strategy used in highest diplomacy!) As an example, while dressing the protesting and wriggling youngster, after you have let him have his say ("No!") and he has convinced himself that he has made an impression on the world, he will most likely cooperate amiably and do what is asked of him.

There will be other moments when this beguiling toddler lays on the charm with a trowel, and at those moments you will get some idea of how loving he can be, and how much the love he has received has been deeply rooted. And it is startling to think of how far he has come in turning into a "person" in the short time since babyhood.

Meanwhile, as you continue to whisk your child out of danger's way, he can begin to learn, even if he cannot understand the "why" just yet (this comes a little later), that it must be "here," not "there." Granted this is easier said than done, but if a child is pleasantly distracted, if you talk about something else or offer a substitute object—"*this* one, not *that*"—he can still get the message that you mean business and firmly expect him to follow your directions. When we are offered a compensation, some substitute for what we must relinquish in life, we are helped to go through many hardships and sacrifices. And life is a series of giving up one satisfaction but gaining another. For most humans, however, it is mighty difficult to give up any great pleasure voluntarily without knowing that something equally enjoyable is there to replace the loss. For the toddler it is almost impossible.

SPECIAL PARENTAL HANGUPS

This human being in the making, this budding little individual, now has to learn the trick of pleasing his parents *and* himself at the same time. This neat trick is actually a lifelong task for all of us in regard to those we love, but it results in our ability to compromise, to give and take. This task is always easier for those of us whose parents did not expect too much of us too soon, but rather showed their loving appreciation for each of our attempts to please them and to conform to their necessary but not overwhelming demands.

From this point on—maybe earlier, maybe later—through many years to come, our children's behavior and problems may stir up all kinds of miserable feelings in us, some of which are related to our own difficulties as young children, even if we are not always able to connect them. We often go through a few of our own battles; sniped at by uncomfortable feelings when our children suck their thumbs, masturbate, dawdle, wet and soil, have temper tantrums, etc.—all part and parcel of growing up. Some of these uneasy feelings are unconscious, and others vaguely conscious memory traces of those earlier days, bringing us back to childhood experiences with our own parents.

One of these unconscious or half-conscious pressures is a tendency in many of us to look for or even see our own worst "faults" in our children. We fear that those faults will prove we are failures as parents, and/or that our children will somehow, through their unattractive behavior, expose our own weaknesses to the world. And matters are not improved when our neighbor smugly announces, "Alice *never* has temper tantrums. What about Mary?"

The Roots of Love

At such upsetting moments, caring about the opinion of our neighbors, naturally we may quickly jump into action to nip in the bud our child's unpopular behavior, or a behavior tendency we dislike or reject in ourselves. And, even stranger than this, we often use the very same method of trying to correct the behavior that our parents used with us, which did not "work" and which caused us unnecessary suffering and shame besides. (It also seems a paradox that we should expect perfection in our children when we aren't perfect, and that we feel they should quickly circumvent the same problems we had so much trouble with as children.)

The following are a few examples of "doing to others what was done to us."

Betty is clingy and shy and quiet, not at all "outgoing." Betty's mother was just like this as a child, and was pushed by her parents into social situations she hated and that did her no good. Yet Betty's mother—not too aware of what she is doing—pushes *her* child. We also seem to forget a few other things. It makes little sense to type-cast a child so young. A child may be shy and reserved at one stage of development, and at another point in his or her growth reverse her "type." Furthermore, some quiet, shy people are capable of having deep and lasting emotional attachments in adulthood, and some are not. By the same token, some outgoing people are capable of loving deeply, too, and some are not. (This capacity has more to do with character and less with personality.)

Junior, aged twenty months, sucks his thumb when guests arrive. Junior's mother was a thumb-sucker as a child, and was treated harshly. Still feeling some residues of guilt and shame from those days, she roughly pulls his thumb out of his mouth and scolds him.

Tony has the same pigheadedness that caused his father so much grief in *his* childhood. Tony's father, nevertheless, meets his son head-on in a battle of wills just as he was met by his parents.

Dr. Therese Benedek has observed that parents get another chance to resolve some of their earlier struggles with themselves and with their parents just through being parents. Sometimes old

The Toddler's Love Affair with the World

conflicts may be "worked through" during the years of mothering and fathering as the parents try to help their child overcome similar conflicts. Being more perceptive now, a mother or father may gain new insight into some of the whys of the unhappiness he or she *and* the child may be experiencing.

Now and then we can stop ourselves short when we get to an impasse with our very young child, and try to see what is really going on between the two of us. We may be able to perceive, for example, that the shame and guilt and outrage and frustration we often feel, besides the anger we direct toward our child, may be the same defensive emotions we felt so long ago when we were being scolded and chastised by our parents. Such insights may help to give us a fresh look at our children, give us a chance to see them more objectively, and *enjoy* them more. In addition, rather than having to repeat and repeat the fruitless old ways of dealing with their problems, we may find it easier to try a new approach and see what happens. Perhaps, too, by relaxing somewhat in attempting to live up to unrealistic standards of perfection in ourselves and in our children, we can learn to become good parents to *ourselves*. Then we can become good parents to our children.

One young mother was reminded of her own struggles for independence as her twenty-month-old kept repeating "No!" These struggles for selfhood had been a lost cause until many years later, when she received psychological help. As a toddler, she conveyed her message not only with her verbal "no's" but also with her body language by frequently and firmly stamping her foot. Her mother, shocked and aggravated by this behavior, and fearful she was raising a "naughty, willful brat," responded by warning the child, "Don't you *dare* defy me! Don't you *dare* stamp your foot and answer me back. I am going to break that will of yours and show you who is boss!" With the self-knowledge she gained in therapy, the child, now a mother, was able to avoid repeating this unhappy pattern with her own toddler. While managing to keep her little daughter within firm boundaries, she still gave her ample room within those boundaries to express her *feelings* and to declare her toddler "independence." (Note: One does not always need therapy to become aware that certain kinds of disciplining we received may have been pernicious. And while we are not always able to recognize the reasons behind our responses and actions, it may help at least to try.)

None of what has been said means you will always be serene and composed and able to manage each little problem with your child as it comes up. Nor does it imply that your child is going to bypass his share of the problems of growing up. But it *may* mean that at his worst moments, some of the heat of your anger will be off so you can remain at simmering instead of at boiling point. As you learn to check your anger to a degree—knowing more about what makes him act so desperately—your child is apt to learn eventually to check *his* anger to a degree also. All of this will be explained in further detail shortly.

IS THIS BEING "PERMISSIVE"?

To this writer, "permissive" is a label usually tacked onto parents who give their children some freedom of choice, who have respect for their dignity—even in toddlerhood—and who are able to guide their children by love and faith and encouragement rather than through fear and anger and punishment. However, if parents set up no controls or limits, deny their children nothing, build no structure, schedules, or routines into their daily lives, this is no longer "permissive." It is *indulgence*, license, or—at its worst—neglect.

Every parent will "permit" his child to do certain things at times and limit him at others. A permissive parent—in the best sense of this unfortunate and much abused word—can permit his or her child "to act his age" when very young, yet not approve of this same behavior when he is somewhat older. He or she is flexible enough to know that one child may need to be held by fairly firm reins while another child needs to be given more slack. And this parent knows that as each child becomes more responsible for himself and more mature, these reins may be further loosened.

To return to our toddler. At eighteen months or so, he

The Toddler's Love Affair with the World

certainly has heard *you* cry out "No!" *He* hasn't invented the word. Yet if you can save your ammunition for the "no's" that are really necessary, you will find that your child is apt to catch on quickly that you mean it at those times. He is far more likely to comply, albeit with some resistance. If, on the other hand, he is constantly bombarded by "no's," you can be sure he will be less inclined to hear or pay attention to the important ones. Furthermore, it is quite possible he may get the impression that everything he does is dangerous or "bad." This can take the wind out of his sails just at that precious time when he is learning to do things for himself, and at a time when he is experiencing the joy of touching, feeling, and testing.

Now this certainly is not suggesting, for example, that the toddler be left to run amuck and turn the living room into a shambles, or take over the personal property or rights of others, or "run" the parents, or get into danger.

One set of parents, aware that at this age their child was beginning to learn about "me" and "mine" and "you" and "yours," felt that as part of his gaining an identity he needed to have some space and place in the living room that he could call his own. Therefore, when he made a lunge for their books on the bookshelf, they lifted him up gently and said, "No, Bobby, these books are Mommy's and Daddy's. Here are *your* books." They would then place him nearby, where they had set up a little cardboard box containing a few magazines he could pull at and tear up to his heart's content. After a few repeat performances on the part of both parents and toddler, the child began to understand what was meant and he willingly obeyed. Other parents try to toddler-proof the home as much as possible, removing obvious booby traps, temporarily putting aside precious reachable objects from the low tables. When they *have* to yank the child away as he reaches for a lamp or an electric outlet or starts to run out into the street, they do so without making him feel like a Lilliputian delinquent.

In most cases, if a child has interesting objects to handle and places to explore, he gradually learns what objects and places are for him and what are off limits.

The Roots of Love

"HOW AM I DOING?" OR, BUILDING UP SELF-ESTEEM

In the first chapter, there was a brief discussion of how overwhelming feelings of helplessness and powerlessness can lower one's self-esteem and bring out hateful feelings against those who have made one feel this way. These hostile, aggressive feelings can be easily triggered into action. The more that hostile feelings build up, the more they interfere with the child's more lovable qualities. Most certainly there are moments when any child—as with all of us in regard to our loved ones—momentarily "hates" the "bad" mother, as he perceives her at the instant when she must frustrate him. (He begins to feel this way about his father, too, when it is *his* turn to intervene.) But if these "bad" moments and feelings do not come up too often, the child, believing more in his parents' goodness, will continue to believe in his own goodness too, and therefore will want to follow his parents' directives.

The more pleased you are with your child—and with yourself in relation to him—the more you can show this pleasure, the more eager he is to win that pleasure and approval, all of which spells love to him.

The toddler's knowledge that he can make things "happen" strengthens his feelings of competence and his normal, natural sense of "power." Billy has learned to get spoonfuls of creamed spinach to his mouth without spilling it all over the place. Sarah can climb up the stairs and even get down somehow. Dotty searches for her favorite toy in the toy chest and with glee pulls it out. Besides the personal triumph and pride in each of these little achievements—gigantic achievements from the toddler's viewpoint—he relishes the admiration and approval of his parents. "Me do it" may soon become his theme song, but "How am I doing?" remain the unspoken words of the song.

In the days of his infancy, the baby saw smiling, nodding, and approving faces bending over him as his needs were being met. Now, he continues to search for those loving faces. He gets the

The Toddler's Love Affair with the World

answer to "How am I doing?" by the way in which his closest people look at him, touch him, talk to him, value him. He accepts these "judgments," favorable or unfavorable, as if they were the eternal verities. And so he builds up a self-image that usually stays with him throughout life.

"The self may be said to be made up of reflected appraisals," said Dr. Harry Stack Sullivan, one of the founders of the William Alanson White Institute of Psychoanalysis. Unfortunately, even some of the greatest achievers—successful, prominent men and women—take with them into adulthood those early "reflected appraisals": "You're a bad boy (or girl)," "You get on my nerves," "You're just *impossible*," "You'll never learn *anything*"; and the attitudes that usually go with those oft-repeated statements. Such persons often continue to have gnawing doubts as to their capacities despite their obvious success, which they can't seem to enjoy. (Other persons who felt demeaned and constantly disapproved of in early childhood may continue to "fail" at all they attempt, as if to punish themselves for being so worthless, or because their self-doubts restrict or cage their best efforts.) Few of us are always pleased with ourselves, and most of us continue to work at our limitations. But pleasure in achievement is a normal reward to which we are entitled.

"Won't praise and admiration make a child conceited?" asked a mother in a discussion group of parents of toddler-aged children. Another mother added, "And become narcissistic?" And another mother seemed concerned that her child was "just seeking attention."

Over the next few years, in one way or other, whether implicit or explicit, all children call out, "Look at *me! Watch* me!"

Everyone seeks attention. Everyone cries out inwardly at times, "Look at me! Watch me!" But our ways of seeking and gaining attention are more subtle and refined than those of the young child. Young children cannot be politicians, artists, writers, doctors, actors, executives, teachers, Olympic athletes, or flagpole sitters. The resources of the very young are quite limited. Therefore, since they are closer to the expression of their primitive drives and impulses than we, they are somewhat cruder in their methods of attracting notice.

As for "narcissism," a much-bandied-about word these days, it means several things (and, technically speaking, even more). As it is used commonly, it means self-love to an extreme degree—an attitude toward the self that has roots in early infancy. The person who was not cherished at that time may have come to think unconsciously, "Since I am not loved, I shall have to love myself as I would have liked to be loved." This unfortunate human being is often shallow in his relationship with love objects and will easily drift off to new objects who flatter him and make him feel important. Yet this word is not always meant negatively. There is a certain amount of healthy narcissism in each of us, a degree of self-love that enables us to protect our own interests and helps us take pride in ourselves and in our accomplishments.

Down deep inside of himself, the truly "narcissistic" person has a very *low* estimate of himself. He spends a lot of psychic energy in futile attempts to raise this wretched self-image. These are some of the people we think of as conceited, since their vanity seems excessive and they constantly brag about themselves. Forever seeking affirmation, they are the ones whose prototype is the wicked stepmother in the fairy tale "Snow White" who cries out, "Mirror, mirror on the wall, who is the fairest of them all?"

In contrast to the overly narcissistic person, who has great difficulty in relating to other people because he has little real interest in them, individuals with feelings of self-worth ("healthy narcissism") are most likely to be truly interested in other people. Not harassed by overpowering inner needs of their own, they find space for their friends. They are the ones we turn to when we are distressed. We know they will have time for us, time to listen, with empathy and concern, to what we have to say.

A child may seem "conceited," "self-centered," "narcissistic" (and all the other fancy words that some adults will find to describe him at times). But he may have to start off seeming this way to prove himself and to win the acceptance he needs. Although he will be for "Me, myself, and I" for quite some years to come, in time, with all the supports he is given (warm

The Toddler's Love Affair with the World

embraces, words, looks, appreciation, etc.) he is apt to reach that happy state of being when his good feelings about himself will have jelled. Then he no longer will need constant reaffirmation from the "outside." And someday, in adulthood, "he should be able to love another person as he was loved . . ."

SEPARATION FEARS AGAIN—
NEW SLEEP PROBLEMS

Although some toddlers begin to have sleep problems in the first half of the second year (depending upon their alertness to what is going on in their environments), many toddlers, around the second half of this year, begin to make a big fuss about going to bed, or have difficulty in getting to sleep, or wake up fitfully during the night.

Bedtime, for many of us, is a time when, as we lie down, the day's events begin to churn around in our minds. Nighttime often makes all our problems loom larger, and it is the time when we regretfully think of the things that went wrong during the day—the things we *could* have or *should* have said or done. This includes the "esprit d'escalier," which means, figuratively, we think, as we descend the stairs upon leaving a party or ascend the stairs on our way home, of the brilliant remarks we might have made but which didn't occur to us at the proper moment.

In his way, the toddler also experiences regrets at bedtime. It renews his fears of being separated from his mother—and now his father too. This fear coincides with his dawning fear of the loss of their love because he may have done things during the day that displeased them. It also is truly difficult for the toddler to tear himself away at night from the ones he loves so much.

No doubt, the darkness only accentuates and aggravates the feelings of aloneness and separateness, which he would gladly relinquish at this moment in order to be close again to his mother, and safe. (Many adults, too, have a fear of being alone as nighttime approaches and it becomes dark.) This fear of being alone is lessened, of course, if the toddler has a sibling sharing the room. (And so is it with the adult who knows someone is close

The Roots of Love

by.) Moreover, who indeed wants to stop all the fun and games, all the fascinating activities, and turn in when there is so much left over to do? The very expression "turn in" is revealing, since in a way it says that we surrender our autonomy, our self, our control over the self, and let passivity and our unconscious lives take over.

Meanwhile, exhausted parents certainly look forward to a little peace and quiet for themselves and are eager to dispatch their toddler off to his crib or bed with little or no nonsense. And they keep their fingers crossed at the same time, hoping they will not be awakened at night by his calls and, soon, by many requests for that glass of water.

Children of this or almost any age never seem to know when they are weary, and they need adults to help them accept the fact that bedtime is for real. Many parents have found that little rituals help prepare the child for sleep. And when it comes to routines and rituals, very soon children begin to show signs of becoming reactionaries of the first order. They will not let you change *anything* during the ceremonies. They like the status quo, and each step must be followed to the letter. However, have no worry about remembering. If you forget one step or make a slip, you will be reminded of your omission or transgression.

The toddler's tensions can also be reduced somewhat if you show and read to him a "first" picture book (preferably not one with lions and tigers!). Other children are soothed by a lullabye or some other tune from earlier days. Needless to say, the book or song does not matter as much to him as the fact he is getting special attention from his loved ones. After this, if he is tucked in with his favorite blanket or any other "transitional object" close to him, and, best of all, given some loving hugs and kisses, he feels comforted. Often a night light or a slightly open door gives him an extra prop against feeling shut out from his parents into darkness.

Just one more hint. In preparing him for sleep, the more relaxed and tender one can be with the ceremonies (and it is easier said than done when you are in a hurry to get to other things, or go out), the more the reluctant toddler will be helped

The Toddler's Love Affair with the World

to feel he is loved and that all his loved people and things will still be around the following day. Some parents suggest that if you give the child a toy with which to play before he drifts off to sleep, the toy helps to remind him of his daytime life. Another advantage—quite practical too—is that in the morning the toddler may see the toy or toys when he awakens and may play with them quietly for a while before arousing the entire household.

Dr. Katherine M. Wolf and Aline B. Auerbach have written about some of this in their pamphlet *AS YOUR CHILD GROWS: The First Eighteen Months*:

> Beloved toy objects in bed with him give a child a similar feeling of continuing reality; he knows that they too will be there in the morning. Here, if he wants, are things to play with, before he drops off to sleep, or when he wakes—objects which give him something to do, and which, because they are less emotionally charged, somewhat divert him from a constant need for his parents.

Although you are aware of how difficult it can be for the child to retire, stating your position to him that it is time for bed and that you expect him to remain there is more likely to be effective if it is relayed to him clearly rather than in an indecisive way. However, there is hardly a home with very young children that escapes the first, or even second, call for "water." That cup can be brought in goodwill and good faith with a "That's all now. Mommy and Daddy are here in the living room [or will be going out, and Susie is here to stay with you], and you are safe and cozy here in your room. And now good night." It may—or may not—work.

Night waking and nightmares present other problems. One cannot always know the reason why little children call out, and there may be one of several physical reasons: fevers, a pain somewhere, the eruption of a new tooth, soiled diapers that feel uncomfortable, etc. But more often there are psychological reasons which, at best, one can only try to sort out and then attempt to handle.

The Roots of Love

We know babies dream and may wake up in terror, screaming. When toddlers go through this experience, their dreams may indicate one of two things—or both. The child may have been overstimulated during the day in ways that are beyond his capacity to absorb and integrate. This being so, he needs to be helped to slow down and take it easy. Maybe he needs to have longer rest or quiet play periods. The second cause for his nightmares may be the beginning of dreams so common to children under six or so—dreams of lions and tigers, witches and ogres, and other ferocious beasts. These frightening images may represent disguised images of the child's parents, whom he loves and also fears. They may also be connected with his own feelings of anger toward them, which he fears they suspect.

Of course, this kind of wakening means that You (Mother or Father) would want to come into the dreamer's room, sit down with him next to or on his bed, pat him gently, murmur soothingly that all is well. This may take a bit of doing, and sometimes one needs to hold the child close to help calm and reassure him in what may be his half-sleep. Some parents—all too well-meaning—believe they should take the child into their bed at such moments. Even though the child may want this very much, such moves usually create more problems than they solve. The child may enjoy this experience so much that he is apt to continue to kick up a fuss in the evenings in order to gain a repeat performance.

One other problem mentioned more fully in the previous chapter may arise again now. When you plan to go out in the evening, do try to leave *after* the child has come to know his sitter—even if this takes a half-hour or so. Likewise, if you leave without telling him you are going out (as with the baby who was so upset) and he awakens to find a strange face instead of yours, he is bound to feel he has been abandoned. The experience may only increase the feelings of uncertainty and insecurity that have made him wake up time and time again. Despite his objections (which may continue even past his third year), what you are doing now by planning your exits so carefully is to build up his continuing trust in you and belief in himself.

The Toddler's Love Affair with the World

Just as a turtle pulls way into his shell for protection, a young child sometimes retreats temporarily to protect himself against things in the environment that may seem too much for him. This means, as has been said previously, he may want a bottle at nighttime after he has given it up. It may mean he drags his blanket (or whatever) with him all day long, or, if he was toilet-trained early, finds it easier to wet and wear diapers again. And so it goes all along the lines of what you have thought was permanent progress. Somehow, these temporary "regressions" seem to give him the inner rest he needs and time to gather new strength to push forward once again when he feels ready. These backtrackings occur sometimes when a new baby appears in the family, when someone in the family is ill, or during or after any family crisis or upheaval which may have affected him.

His periods of babyish behavior may occur even more often during his third year, when he will be learning so many new things, and when so much more will be expected of him. Since we know that "behavior is the language of the child," we can only do our best in trying to interpret what he is trying to tell us. Usually patience, empathy, and understanding on our part, and some lessening of our demands on him for a while, may help him renew his thrust to go forward again.

THE TWO- TO THREE-YEAR-OLD

CHAPTER SEVEN

Learning Impulse Control Through Love

CONTROL OF BOWEL AND BLADDER

Some readers may well wonder why the issue—if it must be an issue—of toilet "training" is being discussed in the two- to three-year-old section rather than earlier. Others may wonder what possible connection there is between love, bowels, and bladder.

Let us take up the first question first.

Many of today's young parents seem to show little concern over the matter of dry pants until their child has reached about two or two and a half. One mother revealed that "Tommy wasn't at all interested in going to the toilet until about his third birthday, when he learned he could soon go to nursery school, but only if he was able to give up diapers and wear pants. He then got busy and became dry in a few days."

The new relaxed trend may have been furthered by the fact that disposable diapers are now available in extra-large, toddler size. At any rate, many pediatricians and psychiatrists back up this more-relaxed attitude (or maybe they started it) and feel there is almost no good reason to ask a youngster under two years of age to hold back his flood gates and wait, or to ask him at other times to open them. One psychiatrist, Dr. Theodore Lidz, feels that a host of difficulties for both mother and child may be somewhat circumvented through postponing this step. He goes so far as to say, ". . . premature training imposes demands that the child cannot readily master or even understand before the age of two and a half or three."

This statement may well startle some. But before taking up Dr. Lidz's argument, a word of reassurance for those who have begun their baby's toilet-training earlier.

Early Versus Later Training

Your grandmother probably began placing her baby (your mother, father, mother- or father-in-law) on the potty at about nine months—or even, for some, at two or three months of age. Your parents' generation started with you perhaps at a somewhat later age—most likely about twelve months, or perhaps fourteen. Then, gradually, the age recommended for starting the process advanced to about eighteen months or so. And now this!

Yet even today, in our country and all over the world, the teaching of bladder and bowel control varies from an age that we might consider much too early to an age that we might presume is much too late. Millions of children have grown up quite well under such diverse systems, while others haven't. The key to the problem seems to be not the timing, but rather the relationship between "trainer" and "trainee." When the teaching process takes place gradually, gently, with a mother's sensitive understanding of her child's responses—just as when she fed and weaned her baby—the *time* at which it is initiated becomes less important psychologically. Whether early or late, when a mother and child get into a hassle over bowel and bladder control, becoming enmeshed so intensely in conflict that the matter becomes a victory or defeat at each round for either of them, there is likely to be trouble ahead.

"Training" seems such an inappropriate word here. You "train" a dog to be housebroken. With a child, such complex neuromuscular, emotional and intellectual capacities come into play that it makes the whole thing a different ball game. And children vary, too, in their own attitudes toward being wet or dry. Some dislike feeling wet or soiled even long before they reach the age of two. Others don't mind a bit. Girls seem to become dry earlier than boys. A mother told of her second child,

Learning Impulse Control through Love

a daughter, who disliked having damp diapers. One day, when this toddler was nineteen months, she pointed out that she now was going to use the toidy and wear pants like the rest of the family.

Some children have a regular inner alarm clock for moving their bowels; others have no such inner prompter for "going"—which may be at any time during the day or night. Much depends also on what may be taking place in the home life of the child, experiences that can positively or negatively affect his desire to take a more grownup step.

Even if you urged your toddler to become dry long before the current more-delayed timetable, there is no need to feel you have traumatized him for life. You haven't. If you sincerely wanted your child to be dry at an early age, and you did *not* put the heat on him, and he did *not* seem to oppose you or rebel or show unusual behavior in some other way, you need have little cause for concern.

Nevertheless, it so often happens that when a child is "trained" at an early age, it is the *mother* who becomes trained; she learns to rush her child to the toilet when she believes that certain moment has arrived. The child may "go" at that moment—often through a conditioned reflex, particularly if his bowels or bladder happen to be full—but he will not be a participating partner, or even have much of an idea of what this is all about.

Newer Attitudes

Some of the current thinking goes along these lines: A child's neuromuscular development should have reached a point where he can voluntarily control his bowel and bladder sphincters or muscles, and be able to walk and talk, or give signs that he needs and wants to go.

The "senior toddler" (18–24 months), described in the preceding chapter, has been striving to gain a sense of control over his body, impulses and environment. He also has been wrestling with the task of learning how to please his parents—while not shortchanging himself, either. Considering his added conflicts over autonomy versus separating from Mother, why throw any further struggles into the hopper just now? One also needs to understand that since the baby has largely relinquished his mouth pleasures—taking things "in" through his mouth and sucking—some of his pleasant body sensations are now focused in the anal region, where he has discovered a new source of pleasure: that of releasing and of holding in, and, soon, of discovering he has some control over these functions. At this stage, as Erik Erikson has pointed out, "the child is apt to both hoard things and to discard them, to cling to possessions and to throw them out of house and vehicles." Dr. Erikson also indicates that the child's desire to snuggle with his mother and then push her away is also part of his contradictory modes of "retention and elimination," normal at this age level.

When then should he want to relinquish these still primitive satisfactions until he finds out he has something more important, more gratifying to gain—in this case, being grownup and pleasing Mother?

Many parents know the different ways of introducing the toddler to the toilet seat or potty (this kind of "how to" does not belong in this book). Clearly, then, it is best to wait until the child has begun to understand, is able to and wants to comply—at a time when he "knows" more and "no's" less! Then, perhaps, after he has "acquired and reinforced a core of autonomy," as Dr. Erikson states it, he may decide to use the toilet. After all, in this situation it is the child who is in the driver's seat.

The mother of a two-year-old commented she could not "go through all of that jazz the books tell you of staying right there with your child, lifting her up and down off the toilet seat several times a day when you *think* she has to pee. I haven't the time to watch Sally so closely, yet I don't want anyone else to monkey with her toileting." Instead, this mother who worked part-time made some subtle, casual hints to her child when she was at home with her. And in time, without any fuss, the child willingly complied.

At best, the process goes gradually, and even then does not rate a 100 percent success. "Accidents" are common, particularly

Learning Impulse Control through Love

with the earlier "trained" youngsters. And often, when young children are excited or completely absorbed in their play, their best intentions evaporate into thin air. (They all can do with some reminding.)

As previously mentioned, a child's development never goes along a straight line, and he often takes detours. He may wet again if a new person comes to take care of him; if he is taken to some unfamiliar place; if he goes on a trip with the family, or they move to another home; or whenever there is a crisis of some kind in the home that changes the emotional atmosphere. Various kinds of outer stresses may cause him to take a dim view about becoming or remaining dry. The child often becomes stymied in his efforts because so much of his energy is being used to cope with these other pressures in his life.

A twenty-eight-month-old boy, trying hard to live up to and compete with a very mature five-year-old brother, suddenly decided he too wanted to wear underpants. He was quite proud of his achievement, but when things began to get rough—as he tried in vain to be a shadow of his brother—he reversed his decision. "I don't *want* to be a big boy," he told his parents and, unmiffed, went back to diapers. But there had been other complications in his young life. His mother was well along in a new pregnancy. She had carefully explained to him about the coming event. In looking at her swelling body, he also noticed her gradually disappearing lap space, which meant less room for cuddling. He viewed that baby as a sure threat to his love relationship with her. It was an uphill pull to be a big boy. Maybe it might be easier and more fun to be a baby and to have Mommy and Daddy change his diapers, albeit he insisted on standing up. His parents, well aware that he might take a backslide anyway when the new baby arrived, let him be—while continuing to encourage his growth and sense of competence in other areas. Eventually, as with all children since diapers were invented, he managed to outgrow them.

Wanting to Please Mother

There is an even more basic factor that motivates a young child to become dry—besides wanting to be more grown up—and this

The Roots of Love

has to do with question two at the beginning of the chapter: the love motive.

A young child who has enjoyed a good relationship with his parents (especially his mother or her surrogate, since usually she is the one most involved here) wants to please them, be like them, and take on their ways. One of his rewards for learning how to open and shut his sphincters to suit society (as represented by Mother) is her smile and loving approval. It feels good to go it Mother's way—and now Father's way too. The toddler is learning even more about the rewards of giving to the ones he loves.

On the other hand, Mother need not feel obliged to turn handsprings over his performance and make it such a big deal that he will fear he has seriously displeased her if he has an "accident." Or, should he suspect that his offering to her is so terribly important, he may use the power he has acquired of withholding or giving up to annoy and disappoint her when he is at odds with her. Or still, conversely, to "give" and "perform" only if she is in his good graces at the moment.

When this developmental step of learning sphincter control becomes a power struggle between mother and child, it is quite possible that in adulthood he may "hold back" in tender feelings and love, finding it difficult to "open up," to share, to give and be giving.

You may be a mother who feels she cannot wait until her child is two or so to begin suggesting he might want to follow the example of others in the family and use the toilet. No doubt, then, you are better off *not* following the suggestions offered in this chapter. If waiting this long makes you anxious, uncomfortable, or irritable, your child is apt to feel your basic anxiety and uncertainty, and sensing your *real* wishes—which contradict your good intentions—he may receive one of those mixed messages. However, some of your anxiety about wanting to get along with it may be related to long-forgotten unhappy experiences of your own when you were toilet-trained as a very young child.

Sometimes just a flash of such insight can help a mother relax and be better able to use her real know-how with her child, who,

Learning Impulse Control through Love

after all, is a different person from herself. At least, for those who still feel tense and want to finish with diapering, watch carefully for the sudden development of eating or sleeping problems, increased thumb-sucking, temper outbursts, or unmanageable dawdling. Any of these behavior changes—and you may possibly notice others—may be a cue for you to let down on the "training" for a while. The child may be attempting to adjust to too many things all at once. Or, he may be afraid he will lose your love if he cannot control himself—especially at night, which may account for some of his fears about going to sleep. (And be pleased if there are no problems.)

Postscript: Do not let that neighbor put the screws on you if she comments disdainfully, "What? Johnny isn't *trained* yet?" Stick to your guns even if you are also pressured by close relatives or friends. If you can "buy" this newer, patient, more moderate approach, and are sympathetic to, and tolerant of, your child's inner struggles, he may respond well, knowing his efforts are worthwhile. Your child will benefit, and so will your nerves.

A child's desire to control and manage his body functions, and his feelings of accomplishment as he succeeds, spur him on. At the same time, he is learning to give pleasure to the ones he loves. However, he does need to know that his body output has no bearing on either the loss or gain of this love. Lucky the child who has been treated tolerantly during this time! Eventually, then, he will become tolerant of himself, too, which is a first step toward tolerating others—a truly lovable trait.

CONTROL OF ANGER

When a two-year-old suddenly goes berserk because he cannot have another cookie (tantrums may occur long before this time), and sits down on the floor, screaming and kicking his heels into his parents' freshly waxed floors; or when he bites, scratches, kicks, pushes his mother or father; or tries to snatch, attack, or destroy things in a blind fury, it is enough to make any parental heart sink. "Where is that lovable, loving, considerate little child we are supposed to be raising? Hasn't all our love had any effect on him?"

The Roots of Love

Of course your love has had an effect, even if it isn't showing up at this moment, during the tantrum so typical of this age. What is more, that special bond forged between you and your child—deeply built into his very fiber by now—will be the tool you will be using to teach him right from wrong, to build in him a code of ethics and true values to live by; and it will teach him in time to regard the needs and wishes of others.

Right now he is in a sort of incubation period. All that cherishing he received from both of you will need time to "take." During this period, evidence of these happy results may appear only sporadically. But gradually, almost imperceptibly, more promising signs will appear.

While we have to understand that some children have easygoing temperaments, and some do not display their feelings so openly, the emotions of most young children are raw, naked, and readily combustible.

Dr. Sibylle Escalona, Professor of Psychology, Albert Einstein College of Medicine, reminds us, "Between the second and fourth years of life though, most children feel excitement, pleasure and anger more intensely than at any other time." Angry outbursts and tears come and go like summer thunderstorms that are quickly followed by sunny skies. The tantrum blows away and the child usually reverts to all smiles and giggles, and this while poor Mother's emotions have just gone through a meat grinder. These intense upsets tend to subside in frequency and intensity as the child is helped, and develops the capacity, to find better means of asserting himself and of expressing his distress.

Before discussing some tactics of "handling" these tantrums and other toddler transgressions, let us look at how and why the child ever does learn to toe the line.

Fear of Loss of Love
Around the age of two, the child is still propelled by the "I want what I want when I want it" philosophy, aptly termed by Freud as the "pleasure principle." The child is not born knowing which want is "right" and which want is "wrong"—or when. The restraining but loving parent who represents reality—the "reality

Learning Impulse Control through Love

principle"—has to enlighten the child so that he can begin to learn what directives mean and follow them, and later on be able to follow *inner* directives, be able to live in peace with himself and others, and, to a large degree, accept the rules of the society in which he lives.

Unfortunately for him, at two years of age or so the "graduate" toddler (as one psychiatrist has dubbed him) hasn't acquired a good enough grasp of language through which he can make known his psychic pain. Therefore, his anger, hurt, and frustration are discharged directly via motoric pathways: the tantrums, kicks, etc. Soon enough he begins to fathom, as mentioned earlier, that his parents aren't exactly enchanted with him when he dashes his plate onto the floor. Even though he doesn't yet know *why* this behavior upsets them, their reproachful looks, voices, and words make him feel uneasy, uncomfortable. Has he lost their love? he wonders in fear.

Up to now, the child's deepest fear has been of losing his love object: Mother. And these early separation fears are not yet overcome, either. Now, on top of this, a new fear has entered into his being: that of losing her *love,* and Father's love too. These fears are not clearly distinguished from each other. They are closely interwoven.

The thought of losing this love is most chilling and terrifying to a very young child—even more if he has had a good share of it. To be unloved is the equivalent of being rejected and consequently abandoned. (This fear remains with all of us to some degree in our love relationships, throughout adulthood, but it does not dominate us as it does the helpless child. Should we be rejected or abandoned after having been deeply attached—painful and shattering as it may be to both our sense of self and to our emotions—we eventually pick up the pieces and move on to newer horizons.)

Underlying the child's fear of both separation from his parents and the loss of their love is his terror of being left alone and unprotected. ("Who would take care of me?")

If the toddler's parents have been loving *most* of the time (and to repeat, parenthood cannot be all patience, wisdom, love, and

The Roots of Love

tenderness; we are only human, and we sometimes yell and scold and act against our better judgment) and if the toddler has had his way and say a good share of the time, he basks contentedly in the warmth of their love. He feels "good" and loves himself as he believes they love him. When he realizes he has done something "bad," he soon begins to sense the chill of their disapproval, and maybe their anger too. At such times he doesn't love himself either; his self-esteem takes a nose dive. His uncomfortable feelings—now felt as anxiety—later will become guilt feelings. Guilt is the voice of conscience.

We adults know only too well how unpleasant and uncomfortable guilt feelings can be, and we like to avoid experiencing them. Dr. Edith Jacobson, psychiatrist and psychoanalyst, explains that the conscience doesn't just disapprove of certain acts or impulses, "but may morally condemn or praise the total self." For example, we are rewarded by our conscience and feel great when we have come to the aid of someone in need, and when we ignore his plight (being "too busy" or not wanting to be involved or whatever excuse we can find), we can't help but think less of ourselves as we feel the pangs of guilt.

The child, then, has a choice. He can, for instance, make a grab for the telephone that Mommy has said was out of bounds. But, should he succumb to this temptation, he may experience some anxiety. An inner signal will flash telling there will be a falling out with Mommy and she won't be loving him.

Or, he may try to resist his impulse—a truly great accomplishment for a tiny tot, since his inner breaks are still quite weak and he cannot always stop himself—and he relinquishes the pleasure of playing with the phone. However, he will feel better about everything; his anxiety will be allayed, and he has the satisfaction of knowing Mommy will approve of him and continue to cherish him. Then he can love himself too.

Soon he may feel uneasy while doing something he knows he shouldn't be doing, even when Mommy isn't around to catch him at it. (He may look sheepish as he touches the phone hesitantly, and may decide to pull away quickly or remind himself by saying, "Tommy not touch.") As he gets to be a little

Learning Impulse Control through Love

older, he will feel uncomfortable at times just for *thinking* about doing something forbidden. By this time the child will have learned a good deal more about how to restrain himself and put off the immediate fulfillment of his wishes so he may enjoy a less tangible but more enduring reward.

Most adults function on this principle. We know that if we acted on all of our impulses, the results for us and for everyone else would be sheer chaos. So we tend to think of consequences—for the future as well as for the present. We think of long-range solutions, and we compromise. Often we forego pleasure of the moment in the interest of what lies ahead, and it is a struggle that remains with us for as long as we live. Furthermore, we too will often relinquish satisfying some of our wishes and whims to please the loved person and to retain his or her affection.

The child not only imitates his loved parents through identifying with them and taking into himself some of their beliefs and characteristics, but soon he takes on their ideals. Through this process he develops an ideal self to strive for, and a conscience. This conscience, which has its start in these early years, *develops only through the child's ability and opportunity to form a meaningful attachment to at least one loving, caring person.* Without anyone to love there is no way for a child to develop a conscience. And the person who grows up without feeling any guilt over wrongdoing is in trouble. He is likely to become a psychopath; someone without a conscience. Indifferent as to the consequences of his acts, for himself and for others, he cannot or will not follow any laws. In extreme cases he may end up in the world of criminals and become one of those who is ruthlessly violent and brutal without experiencing a qualm.

But a conscience can also be too severe and may restrict and inhibit healthy personality growth. The child's behavior, lacking the spirit of adventure and healthy assertion, is apt to be bound by fear—fear of blame and severe scoldings, from without and from within himself.

Yet, if parents are fair and reasonable, and have some compassion for the toddler and his inner battles, letting him act his age and not expecting too much from him, the chances are good he will develop a fair and reasonable conscience. This conscience will work *for* him and not *against* him. It will become his friend and guide—not his dictator. It lets him have some fun.

Using Love as a Weapon

On a city street, a mother was threatening her exhausted little two-and-a-half-year-old, who by now, tired from walking, was screaming and begging to be picked up and carried. "If you behave this way, I'll leave you right here and go away!" the mother exclaimed angrily, shaking the child.

There are some who, often unknowingly, use love not as a tool but as a weapon. "Do this for Mommy to show her you love her." Or, they may say, "If you don't behave I won't love you any more." Sometimes, with the best of intentions, the parent unwittingly gives and asks for the gift of love, but attaches strings to it. The child is apt to get the idea that you appease the one you love, and only then are you loved. This is quite different from wanting the loved one's approval, or *wanting* to please her. It is also emphasizing only too clearly to the child that his deepest fears of being unloved or deserted for an infraction of some rule or behavior are justified. Here we can see the blocking of the child's later confidence in knowing it is possible to be loved and to love unconditionally—just because he is he or she is she.

And when a parent threatens, "If you are bad I will go away and leave you"—as with the little two-and-a-half-year-old—the child may begin to conform at a great price to his selfhood ("I'll do just *anything* to be loved and not abandoned"). Although we know there are many timid souls in this world, some of them have become overly "good," acquiescent, and dependent through anchoring these fears. Many of them have just bottled up their resentments, which may explode later in life in various indirect and surprising ways.

Likewise, those parents who declare "I won't talk to you for a day" are also threatening to shut off love and leave the child stranded and helpless. More than this, Dr. John Bowlby believes that a mother's use of threats to abandon her child in efforts to discipline him may be a tactic that has more of a harmful effect

Learning Impulse Control through Love

on a child than is now known. He writes, "There is reason to believe such threats play a far greater part in increasing a person's susceptibility to separation anxiety than has been realized by psychiatrists."

There are other ways in which "love" can be misused in negotiations with a very young child. One of them is by rewarding a child constantly for "good" behavior by giving him new toys and by depriving him of the toys when he is "bad." ("For having done this you cannot have that bike for Christmas," etc.) When a child *repeatedly* meets this giving and depriving, it is easy enough for him to begin to equate the acquisition of objects with love and being loved. You are "good" and you "get." Possessions (the toys) represent love and the lack of them means being unloved.

No one questions the parental right and joy of giving their child presents, spontaneously or thoughtfully or "just because," or even as a recognition of some exceptional accomplishment. Like most matters, it is all a question of degree.

Unfortunately, a child can also play this game, when he is somewhat older, against his parents, for all it is worth. "I'll do what you want, *if* you promise to give me a . . ." And we all must know people who continuously buy clothes and objects for themselves for which they have little or no need. The new purchases, whatever they may be (and we are not speaking of art and antique collectors, etc., for which the object may have a quite different meaning), helps to give them an illusory sense of being enveloped and surrounded by love.

Handling the Anger and Tantrums

Returning now to our two-year-old's tantrums. The parent who can avoid locking antlers with the toddler in a counter adult tantrum (and it is an adult feat to remain calm under these circumstances) will be helping the child to learn several things:

- If he sees that you are not hurt or frightened by his anger and his wish to strike out—the strength of which may scare him too—he may realize through your quiet yet firm

The Roots of Love

response that you are there to help him master these unwelcome expressions of his feelings. He also feels relieved that he is being helped through being held back.
- He will soon learn that you are not going to let him hurt himself or others, or wreck their property. "Yes, Johnny, I know you *feel* angry. But you may not hurt the table or yourself or other people. Come on now, let's do something else." By the time he is somewhat older one might add, "Tell me why you feel so angry and let us *talk* about it."
- You show him that he has a right to experience any kind of feeling, but that there is quite a difference between *feeling* and *acting out* that feeling.
- By not giving in to the request—as with the cookie, for example—once the tantrum has started, he learns that the tantrum leads nowhere. His behavior is not rewarded.

The kicking child can be gently but firmly restrained (yet, as with swaddling, some children find this restraint calming, others do not; however the restraint still "tells" him something). Or, if the child is bothering others, he can be lifted, struggling and kicking, into another room until he has calmed down. And when he yells "I hate you!" don't be shocked or take it to heart. Maybe he does "hate" you for a split-second—all the while hating himself too. You are of course the "bad" and frustrating mother, but soon—at about three or three and a half years of age, according to Dr. Margaret Mahler—the child begins to realize that the "good" and "bad" mother are one. As he grows up, then, he may learn not to expect perfection in the woman of his dreams! (A woman may learn not to expect perfection in her man, or in herself, for that matter.)

Aside from these suggestions, one can only try to figure out what really brought on the temper tantrum. That cookie, obviously, may just have been the last straw. What is the child trying to tell you through this unhappy behavior? Finally, you can try to avert or divert the tantrum when you feel it is heading your way. But total success is just an idle dream. No matter what you try to do at times, the spark just bursts into flames. With it

Learning Impulse Control through Love

all, the child does need some reassurance after the tantrum is over that all love is not lost between you.

In the course of time, some of his angry, aggressive feelings begin to merge with the love feelings that have expanded within him, making it possible for him to redirect his anger into different channels. Drives need expression through *some* satisfying form or other. Given help, a child soon discovers there are many acceptable ways in which he can express these drives and still have fun. He sublimates, pounding at clay and at peg boards, hammering, driving off fast in his "car." He messes with sand and water, he rearranges his "world" to his suiting through pretend play with little dolls and little "people." He uses words, fantasy; he creates and listens to stories—all of which help him to get rid of some of his angry feelings and which bring him pleasure besides.

As he reaches three, the "graduate" toddler will continue to slip up from time to time and seem to go to pieces—particularly when tired, hungry, or not feeling well, or when his attempts to overcome some obstacle in his play (work) have failed. (And we adults are certainly not at our best under any of these circumstances, either.)

The more you can show pride in the toddler's steps toward self-control, the stronger will be his desire to succeed further. Soon, he finds an even wider variety of acceptable ways of redirecting his strong, negative, or hurt feelings. These new vents or escape hatches give him not only greater enjoyment and feelings of accomplishment, but also bring him rewards through his parents' delight in him. He will be working now toward making those few but necessary rules that you have set up for him a part of himself. And ultimately, he will strive to develop an ideal self and a workable conscience too.

CONTROL THROUGH SPANKING?

Most likely there are few parents who haven't at one time or other given their young child a swift smack or swat or whack—or come pretty close to it. And while there are some parents who would not dream of hitting a child under any circumstances, there are many more, unfortunately, who believe that corporal punishment "will teach him to mind." It is a sorry sight when parents, nursemaids, and housekeepers in parks, playgrounds, supermarkets—most anywhere—push, pull, shake, slap, and spank even the tiniest.

This kind of "teaching," however, doesn't teach a child "to mind," but it does teach him a number of other things. He is apt to learn that:

Might Is Right
When a mother attempts to teach her young child to curb his angry impulses, making it clear that he may not hit or attack others, and then strikes *him,* she is doing the very thing she is telling him *not* to do! Not realizing this perhaps, the "teacher" is actually sanctioning physical aggression and physical violence. At such moments a very young child may be shocked and terrified to discover that Mother, or Father, is not his protector against physical harm, but rather his attacker. The child, who cannot retaliate *now* due to his size and bodily weakness, may begin to harbor feelings of deep resentment and humiliation. By identifying with the angry and aggressive side of his parent, the child, when bigger, may let out his need to get even by bullying and attacking smaller, more helpless youngsters. (In extreme cases, these unspent, resentful feelings may be vented on society through physical violence of one kind or other.)

Spanking can deeply wound a young child's pride. Even at two or three, it is an invasion of the youngster's body and spirit, a violation of his integrity, rights, and personal dignity. "The wound to the child occurs," according to Dr. Sylvia Brody, "even when no physical pain results, because the physical assault violates the boundaries of control and physical separateness."

Sometimes parents will argue, "*I* was spanked as a child and it didn't do *me* any harm!" Dr. Selma Fraiberg has answered this one nicely by saying, "I suspect that deep in the memory of every parent are the feelings that had attended his own childhood spankings, the feelings of humiliation, of helplessness, of submis-

Learning Impulse Control through Love

sion through fear." For this reason, along with others, most parents have misgivings, guilt, and remorse after having struck their child.

The Development of Conscience and Spanking

As we have seen, in his third year the toddler begins to feel uncomfortable, and soon experiences twinges of guilt for having gone counter to his parents' bidding. Strangely enough, should he be physically punished, his guilt feelings may be bypassed—if he is already aware that he is misbehaving. His guilt is relieved because he has paid for his escapade. He is squared off by the spank! The child is free now to get into mischief again. Johnny's philosophy is well on the way to becoming "I'll buy now and pay later." So he lunges for the phone, which is forbidden territory, and in a real sense gets off scot-free. In time he leans heavily on the rules and penalties that come from the outside world (the outer controls) instead of those that come from within himself (the inner controls), the latter being the conscience which tells him when to stop and why.

Common Misconceptions About Spanking

"HE'LL LEARN NOT TO DO 'THAT' AGAIN." A twenty-two-month-old toddler was happily running along a city block. His parents, pushing his empty stroller, were busily talking and failed to see him go off the curb. By some miracle, a taxi barely avoided running into him. The distraught father grabbed his child and began to beat the daylights out of him while the innocent, bewildered, and shocked youngster screamed in wild terror and misery.

One can sympathize with the toddler's parents, knowing how frightened and upset they were. No doubt they must also have felt guilty realizing they should have kept a closer watch on their child, who obviously was not yet ready to walk alone on a city street. But how could the release of their anger and guilt upon the child have helped him learn anything but fear and resentment of them, and insecurity and confusion about himself?

When a child, such as this one, is too young to reason with or understand the directives he is given—not yet able to relate cause and effect—he is usually too young to understand *why* he is being spanked. A yank at this age is better than a spank. At least he may be able to understand when he is being pulled away from something or someplace that this thing or place is *verboten*.

"It will clear the air." As one psychologist commented, "A fusillade of bullets will also clear the streets." Sometimes a toddler will be scared out of his tantrum—for the time being—into submission and silence, but the air soon becomes congested again. Eda LeShan, noted family-life educator, lecturer, and writer, declares that spanking "may relieve our anger and may clear the air . . . but it does not teach constructive lessons about human relations, and after all, that's what discipline is all about; the ways in which we teach our children to live in a civilized fashion with themselves and others."

"He's asking for it." When a child's behavior seems to provoke the physical punishment he dreads, it may be time to discover *why*. Is he attempting to get the attention he feels is going to his older or younger sibling, and does he somehow, even through the spank, feel he is getting the notice he craves? There may be other reasons, some of which go deeper. Occasionally a child derives a certain pleasure out of his pain or humiliation. If you are puzzled or sense there is more here than you can understand, rather than "letting him have it," it is wiser to pick up this danger signal and seek some skilled professional counsel.

"He'll learn to respect me." By now the reader must surely be more than familiar with one of the themes underlined in this book suggesting that mutual feelings of trust, respect, affection, and enjoyment are what build up a good relationship between parent and child, despite the inevitable difficult times. Spankings can throw a wrench into this growing relationship and block off the flow of open and honest communication that will soon be developing between parents and child. A sensitive young child who is spanked may become so fearful and distrustful of his parents that he withdraws his wish to confide in them over the years. He may also learn to evade, tell half-truths instead of the whole truth, go "underground," and even deliberately lie to

Learning Impulse Control through Love

escape the physical blows. (We all surely know of some adults who resort to these methods of avoiding blame and responsibility for transgressions.)

A few final words: Hardly any parent who has spanked his or her child is necessarily a mean, cruel, unfeeling tyrant (and that goes even for many of the child abusers we read about who may have suffered untold miseries and abuses in their own childhoods, and who are more in need of help than of condemnation). Although spanking is an open admission of parental defeat and failure—and often the child senses this too—there may come a time when a parent's patience has worn thin. Following a day of irritations, frustrations, and stresses (and this may include years of accumulated private hells and pains), when Johnny or Mary drops Mommy's or Daddy's wristwatch into the toilet, or scatters the contents of the salt container all over the apartment or house, this may be *it*—and *wham!* Nor have parents who resorted to hitting their child now and then necessarily done irreparable harm, unless this hitting has been their continued approach to the child's undesirable behavior. It is still early enough to stop this truly unworkable and potentially harmful form of discipline. Children have remarkable strengths and abilities to recover from occasional parental mistakes. When the bonds between parent and child are sound and loving, an infrequent swat is not unlikely to undo them. *But the swats are not apt to help these bonds strengthen, either.*

From now on, as you teach your child to become a thoughtful, loving, considerate human being, it may be helpful to bear in mind the definition of discipline offered by Aline B. Auerbach, family-life educator and author. "Discipline," she says, "is something you do *for* and *with* the child—not *to* him."

LEARNING TO COPE WITH JEALOUSY AND RIVALRY

Child-rearing styles may change just as life styles may change, but ever since the time of Cain and Abel, children have had to face the bitter pangs of jealousy, envy, and rivalry. Unfortunately for these brothers, Cain and Abel's parents hadn't been briefed on "sibling rivalry"! (Rivalry, in terms of children, really means the competition and fight that develop between them for access to, and priority with, Mother and/or Father. Part of the ancient derivation of the word itself is somewhat similar: two tribes on either side of a stream or river, or *rivus,* would fight for *their* rights to its access.)

Even the awareness of this affliction, however, isn't too helpful when you run smack into the situation with your child. What is more, you cannot protect your first-born from experiencing distressing feelings of jealousy when his or her new brother or sister is born, nor can you prevent these emotions from erupting later. Jealousy, just as love, is part of the total range of human emotions that is experienced by mankind. Every one of us meets it in a lifetime; in our social lives, in work, in love. Some of us manage to handle these pains tolerably, some do not fare so well, and others fall apart through them.

Meanwhile, we can help the child to face and accept as natural his strong feelings *now*—when he first experiences them—and help him come to terms with the pangs so that his feelings will not develop into overwhelming and destructive proportions. Instead of battling the nursery fights throughout life for first place with Mommy or Daddy (which is basically what these fights between adult brothers and sisters are all about, regardless of what they are *said* to be about: wide differences of opinion, money, etc.), a child may learn to deal with his childhood (and later, adulthood) jealousies in a healthy, rational way.

Some of the ways in which we can accomplish this are:

Understanding How the Child Feels
Swinging couples notwithstanding, how many couples can stand by calmly and share the affection and attention of a loved one with a rival? Yet here is your first-born, your under-three-year-old, who has been basking in the glory of being an only child.

Learning Impulse Control through Love

During this time he had been the sole delight, the focus of his parents' love and attention. He had been the family's star performer, the one who held the center of the stage. All at once he not only has to share this love, but he has to share the spotlight with an unappealing new starlet who seems to dazzle her audience.

Why should Mommy want another child? the first one may wonder. Wasn't I good enough?

Typically, he may begin to worry that he may have too many shortcomings, since it is not within the reasoning powers of a very young child to believe his parents would have another one if *he* were adequate. Jean Piaget has described the young child's way of viewing the world as "egocentric." This means the child is capable of seeing things only from where *he* sits, and assumes, naturally, that everyone else must see and figure things out just as he does. The senior or graduate toddler is apt to conclude that his parents can't possibly care about him as much as they did before. Without any hesitation, one three-year-old asked his mother plaintively, "Will you love the new baby more than you love me?" Other children, not so outspoken, may show their feelings by being "difficult"—and more about this later.

Preparing the Child

The two- to three-year-old is quite observant, has noticed the bulge of your body (even if he doesn't rudely comment about it), has seen the preparations for the new baby and has heard discussions surrounding the event. (It helps to give the child a sense of active participation in the event by letting him feel the fetal kicks as you explain how the baby is growing inside you.)

Like many other first-borns, he may also have noticed your turning away from him on those days when you were particularly tired or irritable or preoccupied, as one often is during pregnancy. Regardless of how enticing you have made the future happening appear to him, he is inclined to line up against the intruder—the "unknown enemy"—even before he is born. If he is told he will have a baby brother or sister to play with, he may look forward to having a ready-made playmate at hand; he may then have quite a letdown and disappointment when he discovers how things really pan out.

Admittedly, no one can predict just how your older child will react to the dénouement: his first meeting with the baby. He may be curious, be quietly cautious, show a dutiful interest in the baby—or completely ignore him. When you return from the hospital, he may even turn his back on you momentarily, and go on with his business. Should this occur, don't feel hurt. The child may be acting in this fashion because in some obscure way he is angry with you for having left him. Naturally he knew you were going to the hospital to have the baby, but he still didn't quite "know," i.e., admit it to himself.

Fortunately, some hospitals today are aware of the importance, psychologically, for children to see their mothers as soon as possible after the baby's birth. Many of these hospitals make arrangements whereby a mother can come down into the visitors' lounge (some even allow children into the hospital room) soon after the birth for a visit with her older child. The toddler often has harrowing fantasies about Mommy being physically harmed in the hospital. No matter what you have told him beforehand, he is inclined to stick to his own science-fiction version of your hospital sojourn. But just stick to *your* version. By seeing Mommy happy, whole, and well, his anxiety and fears may abate to a great extent, as well as his fears of having been deserted. If hospital visits are out, frequent telephone calls may also reassure the youngster.

Helping the Child Accept His Feelings, yet Curb His Actions

Obviously, no matter how a mother tries, the previously allotted time for her first-born must be cut down. She has only two hands. Naturally, if her older child is only two or under, this may make things only more difficult—but not necessarily so. No matter, it does help to remember that even a three-year-old (who by now may have some investment in activities and life outside the home which do not always involve Mother) still has his normal needs

Learning Impulse Control through Love

to be embraced, touched, and snuggled. In seeing how big he is in comparison to Baby, one tends to forget that he really has not left Babyland too far behind.

Many parents who point out to their older child the compensations of being "big" are sometimes surprised when the advantages don't seem to cut any ice with the youngster. In part, in an unconscious effort to return to his lost paradise, where he enjoyed your exclusive attention, he may slide backward in any of the ways mentioned several times previously. Or, perhaps one day when you are feeding the baby, he may want a bottle too. Should you be breast-feeding he may ask for the breast. You might gently want to tell him that only little babies nurse at the breast, but if he would like it, you might hold him close in the same way as you hold the baby, and let him try a bottle this way—if he thinks he really wants that. "But you will see that the milk tastes better and is easier to get at from a cup when you are thirsty," a mother might add.

While continuing to play up his ability to do things Baby cannot do—skip, jump, run, climb, talk, etc., indicating that all Baby can do is eat, sleep, and cry—it makes good sense nevertheless not to push him. In a certain way he is just marking time to get ready, set, and go—ahead. After he has made his initial adjustment, he may possibly take an enormous spurt in his development. During this period of adjustment, those "special" times just alone with you and certain "special" expeditions with his father and with close relatives, such as a trip to the zoo, a boat ride, or other "grownup" fun, may help him to understand that he really has not been displaced in the family.

Parents can expect most anything from their toddler as he tries out different methods of meeting the situation. When friends and relatives come to visit, he may show off, performing acrobatics, singing loudly, telling a "story," interrupting, doing most anything to capture the stage again and have you see he is pretty cute, too. Let him sing that song, tell one story. A quiet moment on your lap, a loving pat on his head, a suggestion that he might want to draw a picture for you or the "company" or build

The Roots of Love

something with his blocks that everyone can admire, or whatever you can think of, may convince him that he is still on the map. Then you can explain that now you must give your attention to the guest for a while. (If it works!) Another child may act rather withdrawn or be overly "good," trying to sit on his hostile feelings. All children will do well at this time to have an inflatable rubber punching clown, or a peg board, or anything onto which they can pound out their hostilities.

The toddler may express his mixed feelings about the baby— and oh yes, he has loving feelings too for him—by gently patting him or her while also sneaking in a push or a pinch. Or, he may express his disaffection more openly by trying to hurl something in the baby's direction. In restraining him, just as in restraining his tantrums—and part of him does not want to hurt the baby—you again can help him see the difference between *feeling* indignation and *acting* on those feelings. ("Go now and punch Teddybear or Puncho," etc.)

Most of all, the young child does need to know you understand and accept his anger.

In the course of time, the first one may announce one day, "Isn't it time now to take the baby back to the hospital?" And he does not mean for a checkup! Or, as many children have suggested happily, "Let's give Baby to Aunt Mary!" or "Let's dump him into the garbage pail!"

No. Your child is not depraved, but merely voicing thoughts that adults have long since learned to hold in.

LATER REACTIONS TO BROTHER OR SISTER

The new baby isn't always a threat to his older brother (or sister) until he is old enough to get in the way, as he crawls along the floor grabbing toys and knocking over the toddler's blocks. One three-year-old cried out in despair, "Ellen has messed up my parking lot! All my cars were in a row!" And like the egocentric he still is at this age (until he has reached about seven), the older one assumes his younger sibling should know better.

Learning Impulse Control through Love

Soon, it appears, life isn't all that rosy for the second in line, either. Although he has come onto the scene as a second—never knowing what he missed by not being an only child, since he learned to share love right from the start—he discovers he has to fight for his rights too. It is only natural for the bigger one to try to push his younger brother or sister around, who, more often than not, worships his older hero despite the injustices. Although he may be put upon by his older sibling, in time he may catch on as to how to defend himself in a way that comes as a surprise to the older one, who may never have learned self-defense.

Often the littler one longs to be able to do all the things his bigger sibling is capable of, and sometimes pushes himself with all his might in order to catch up. (This can motivate and speed up certain aspects of his development, although as already pointed out, it can also slow it down for a while.) In order that the second child does not become an "also ran," especially if he is of the same sex as the first one, he too needs exclusive attention, special encouragement, and time away from his older sibling—now, and as time goes by.

Ultimately, after a period of varying length during which the first-born has been reassured that his negative emotions are not horrendous and shameful, things do begin to straighten out. In having unleashed some of this steam, room is made for the growth of tender, loving, and protective feelings toward the younger sibling. The time also will come when the two form a coalition against the world—and certainly against their parents! They may hotly defend each other, and find solace in one another's company when they are lonely, especially when parents take a trip.

As your children grow older—although they will squabble, sometimes push and hit and resent each other ("It's *mine*, give it back!" "*I* had it *first!*")—there are apt to be many more moments of closeness, of love, of sharing each other's triumphs, joys, and sorrows. But this won't happen overnight. These ties grow only through years of familiarity and shared experience.

Parents sometimes gain new insights into their children's rivalries and competitiveness by taking a look at their own place

The Roots of Love

in their family of long ago. If you were a second child, you may tend to side too much with the younger one, recalling how you felt being low man on the totem pole. If you were the oldest, you may lean over backward to see that the older child never experiences the jealousy you felt—which, of course, is quite impossible. And, while we usually love all our children with the same *amount* of love, we love each of them *differently*. You may identify more with one child than with another, or find this one easier to be with or more fun to be with. It may make the children happier to know (when they are able to understand) that you love them both the "best" but in different ways. "Sally is special Sally, and Teddy or Edith is specially Teddy or Edith"—or words to that effect.

Like most other children, as yours become more certain about their individual capacities and worth, about their own place under the sun, and most of all in your affections, they will have less need to be jealous of and envy each other. Moreover, as you begin to understand the meaning of your children's trials in dealing with their first intense emotions of jealousy, you will be helping them learn how to share, how to give and take—a basis for loving well.

INFANCY TO THREE YEARS OF AGE

CHAPTER EIGHT

Longer Separations from Parents: Threats to Love

A child begins to develop an emotional tolerance for longer separations from his mother when he is able to visualize her in his mind during her absence. Even after she is gone, her image remains with him. This image, however, is more than just pictorial. It is all that Mother means to the child: her touch, her voice, a look, "that certain smile," a special feeling about her, all of which have become part of him. As Dr. Margaret Mahler explains, the maternal image becomes psychically available to the child "in the same way as the actual mother had been libidinally available—for sustenance, comfort and love." At this point, then, the child has taken another step toward reaching mature adult love, i.e., when the feelings for the loved one remain steady and constant even when the lovers are parted.

There is no bell that rings to announce the arrival of this stage of relative security about the loved object: Mother. Yet the child's successful responses to slightly longer absences from her—at about three years of age, plus or minus—should be some indication of his internal adjustment. Now this does not mean to imply that a child doesn't mind the temporary parting from her, but at least he has more of a capacity to bear with it. Many a three- (and even four-) year-old will still fuss and whine and protest and tell you not to go out, especially in the evening. If it were up to him, he would prefer to have you around all the time.

A. A. Milne, who could so well penetrate the thoughts of young children, illustrates, with his usual subtlety, the child's

The Roots of Love

point of view about separation in a verse called "Disobedience," from *When We Were Very Young:*

> James James
> Morrison Morrison
> Weatherby George Dupree
> Took Great
> Care of his Mother,
> Though he was only three.
> James James
> Said to his Mother,
> "Mother," he said, said he:
> "You must never go down to the end of the town,
> If you don't go down with me."

NURSERY SCHOOL AND SEPARATION

Easing the Child into His New Life

Most experts in child development seem to agree that a child of three, or even some months younger, can benefit from spending a few hours daily at a nursery school, play group, or day-care center. When the situation at home is optimal (attentive mothering person), a child younger than this—in need of so much personalized, individual attention—is probably better off there, either playing alongside another child or sibling (children of this age do not yet play *with* other children), or along with a small group of children in his own backyard or that of a neighbor, or at a playground, supervised in each instance by his mother, another mother he knows well, or some stable mother person.

A child's sense of time develops very slowly, quite late in fact. Being away from his mother for three hours in a totally strange environment may seem like an eternity to a two-year-old, particularly if he is not yet able to console himself with his mother's "image." Yet, there are some two-year-olds who have established ties to persons in addition to their mothers and have frequently visited other homes—*enjoying* the experience—who

Longer Separations from Parents: Threats to Love

now may be ready to take special programs designed for this age group. Other toddlers under three may enjoy just an hour or two once or twice a week in programs with other toddlers. But for the average two-year-old, these ventures away from home may be somewhat of a calculated risk. A parent may have to see how it goes—*if* she can find a good program. (Day-care centers for babies from infancy on and up will be discussed shortly.)

Most nursery schools, however, stay on the safe side and prefer to start with the threes (more or less). They set up programs that begin at nine in the morning and end about noon, five mornings a week.

The three-year-old is taking a tremendous step as he moves away from his secure home base and family to a more impersonal setting on a daily schedule. It is his first introduction to the realities of the outside world, and he has to try to make some sense out of all the strangeness. There is so much that is new to face and to understand; new and strange adults and children, new demands, environment, and activities. The child may be eager to handle all this newness while also fearing he won't be able to swing it. For all of these reasons and others, the best nursery schools do whatever they can to help the child learn to cope with and adjust to his new life.

In the early weeks and months, the aim of the staff is to introduce the child to his external realities rather than to teach him crafts, which he will get later on. Mothers are usually asked to stay with their child for the first few days or week (sometimes longer) until he has become comfortable in his surroundings. (Many summer play groups require the same of mothers.)

As soon as the child seems fairly well acclimated (and this may well be on the very first day, or not until later on), the mother may leave the room, explaining to her child that she will be in an adjacent one if he needs her. The child should have this assurance that his mother is not going to vanish abruptly. Once the child has become acquainted with his teacher or her assistant, he may begin to trust her (or him) and not mind so much when his mother departs—especially if he has been drawn into some activity that has caught his interest. While some

The Roots of Love

children, naturally, take leave of their mothers with differing degrees of reluctance, occasionally a child will panic when it comes time for his mother to depart. And more about this later.

Not all mothers are convinced that such precautionary steps are necessary. One parent saw these measures as "molly-coddling." "It's overprotection!" she declared emphatically.

Once you understand that when a child is *eased* into a potentially threatening situation (and this has already been shown with the much younger child) the situation is likely to become less threatening. These steps, seemingly elaborate and maybe inconvenient too, will also benefit *you*. The strength you are building into your child from the very help you are giving him right now will be carried far into the future. Your love and empathy that now are gently urging him on, yet ready to support him when he rushes back to you, are apt to help him meet the challenge of other separations he may face later on: hospitalization, overnight camp, boarding school, college, etc.

Fortunately, you and your child can communicate well with each other by now, and you can discuss what he might be doing at nursery school beforehand. He may want to hear about some of the activities in which he can participate; he may want to know that the teachers are there to help him and protect him and to show him how to do many things that are interesting and fun. However, it is not necessary to make nursery school sound like paradise or to go into too much detail either, since the child may be disappointed if things are not just as you described them. Perhaps, more than anything, he will want to know when you will return to pick him up.

After overcoming that first real goodbye to Mommy, every little happening in this new world of nursery school that can be mastered gives the child a firmer sense of himself. He will be learning a number of difficult and sometimes painful tasks: taking turns with other children, waiting for that turn, sharing toys and teacher with others, learning how to cooperate and plan with others, learning not to hit or push or shove another child—and learning to stand up for his own rights, too.

Dr. Lois Murphy, who has observed the feelings of triumph

Longer Separations from Parents: Threats to Love

that can come to a little child when he has acquired the capacity to cope with new situations, writes in *The Widening World of Childhood:*

> Each new experience of mastery is not only a momentary conquest but a promise of more to come, a reassurance of the capacity to grow. The sense of mastery is also closely related to a sense of worth, importance, and ability to gain respect from others and maintain one's own self-respect.

And don't these words apply to our own adult lives as well?

When the Child Hesitates

Pushing a reluctant child who clings to his mother usually backfires. When a child is told, "Now be a big boy (or girl) and don't whine and cry," he may only cling more desperately to his mother or whine and cry louder. This admonishing at such a time is like telling a grownup who is feeling upset, depressed, or anxious, "Come on now, pull yourself together!" What parts of yourself *do* you pull together? And how does a very young child with even less of a capacity to know himself or handle himself *not* cry or panic when he is upset or anxious?

Some children will wail loudly or clutch at their mothers when taking leave of them, but many of these same children soon warm up to their surroundings when Mother actually has gone. Other children talk excitedly for weeks about "going to nursery school," and are eager beavers—until the time of parting from Mother. Then there are children who feel more secure when they have taken along some favorite toy or object from home that somehow bridges the gap for them between the familiar and unfamiliar. Even if they just put the toy into their cubby hole and never approach it, it helps them to know the object is there. (The "transitional object" in a new form now.)

Usually, when the child clings to his mother at parting, he chiefly fears what might happen to him while she is gone. However, when a child cannot be consoled and cries even after she has left him, his reasons for suffering may go deeper and are apt to be related to his ambivalent feelings toward her. (The

The Roots of Love

meaning of these deeper fears will be taken up in another section of this chapter.)

Repeated experiences with children have shown that those who have older siblings are inclined to adapt to nursery school more smoothly because they have long heard about school and are eager to copy the patterns of the older one. "Me too!" But should the sibling be younger, especially a new baby, the child may have second thoughts about leaving Mommy! Sometimes he may worry he will lose his place with Mommy by going away to school. And if the school sessions happen to begin very soon after the birth, the child runs into two crises at once: the adjustment to the new baby and the adjustment to school.

Children are so unpredictable. While we may expect a youngster to object under these conditions, some may be delighted to go off despite the new baby. Lisa, aged three, had a close playmate, Paul, who also was going to attend the same nursery school. Lisa was a bit torn between her desire to stay at home with Mommy, to keep an eye on her and the baby, and her desire to join Paul. The girl's father encouraged the part of her that wanted to go into the wider world by suggesting to her, "I'll be going off to my work each day and I'd love to drop you off to *your* work each day." And then he explained that Mommy would take her to school the first week, but after that Daddy would be taking Lisa and Paul to school daily. Lisa voted in favor of school, and Paul and Daddy.

It is not unusual for a child to experience a delayed separation reaction. He may seem quite well adjusted to his school venture, but at home may be irritable and difficult. Or, he may have some fitful sleeping and nightmares, or even wet his pants again. His behavior should not surprise you. The adjustment to school may have drawn heavily on his fund of maturing strength, and he needs to take some time to absorb his experience. He may need to retreat and just "let go." And isn't home the very place where he can do this? To adults as well, home is our castle, where, as a young mother remarked, "You can be yourself 'let your hair down,' so to speak, kick your shoes off, and scratch!"

Should the child's behavior continue to be unusual for an

indefinite period, it may be best either to meet with his teacher, to discuss what the pressures at school may be that cause his tensions, or to consult with a child-guidance worker or family counselor.

Mother's Feelings

Occasionally, a parent's own anxiety about letting her child go comes across to him through her spoken or unspoken words. She may reassure him too much, be apologetic, talk about how they will miss each other every day—even while telling him all about the wonderful nursery school he will be attending. The young child may sense that his mother does not really want him away from her. He may receive another one of those mixed messages that tells him loudly, despite what his mother *says,* that she prefers to have him stay at home.

Even in today's busy and changing world, a mother may at first feel quite lonely and lost as her child begins his life away from her. It may be additionally difficult if she has no challenging interests or work to dig her teeth into, or if there is no younger child at home. Knowing that she has several hours to herself now, a mother may also feel relieved, along with some twinges of guilt for feeling this way. Then, some of us may recall in a vague way, consciously or unconsciously, our own fears and terrors at having been "left" somewhere at some time in our earliest childhood. We may be reliving our own separation fears and experiences, our own anguish about leaving home and facing the unknown. At such moments, through overidentifying with our child, our inner doubts and fears—which can be as catching as the measles or a common cold—are then transmitted to him through amplifiers! At any rate, the perceptive youngster is apt to be aware of the ambivalent feelings that may grip us, and then he digs his heels into the ground when it comes time to depart.

Ambivalence, for you or your child, under any of these circumstances is quite normal. But with the loosening of his ties to you—which have strengthened by now to such an extent that they *can* be loosened—and some resistance on your part in accepting the fact that you won't be needed in quite the *same* way as before, you may also be delighted that your child is starting to grow up, that he is ready to take on a degree of self-reliance, and is ready to deal with the problems that lie outside of the home. And now, a new life for you too.

The mere acceptance of these divided feelings goes a long way in helping you communicate a straighter message to your child, and, as has been said before, to reinforce his own wish to be "big." The keen interest you and his father show in his daily school happenings (at least whatever he wishes to share with you) is apt to further your child's wish to adapt to his new life.

THE WORKING MOTHER AND DAY CARE

Sometimes realities and certain life conditions make it impossible to follow the ideal plans, and one has to seek alternative solutions. What if a mother works and can find only makeshift arrangements for her child that she inwardly believes will be inadequate? She may even know of an available stand-in for her, but also realizes that her child is now ready for some intellectual and social stimulation. What, then, if she cannot afford nursery school* for her three-year-old or even a child somewhat younger than this?

The question of alternatives is basically a question of what is available. What is best for the child? What choices are still open to the mother? If she is lucky, she may be able to find part-time work, and if her child is under three she may happen to have a husband whose own work schedule or type of work makes it possible for him to care for the toddler a few hours daily. She might even know some other mothers with similar needs—and most important, with attitudes and knowledge about children that match hers—who could form a baby-sitting cooperative. In such a co-op (and there are many varieties of baby-sitting cooperatives in which groups of mothers work out satisfying arrangements), each of, say, five mothers could take turns

---

* Some communities have cooperative nursery schools where fees are lowered in return for mothers' occasional assistance to the staff.

Longer Separations from Parents: Threats to Love

looking after the other four children, the better part of a day or half day once a week. Activities are planned for the children, and if they stay through part of the afternoon, they are given lunch followed by a nap. All of which gives each of the other mothers four free days (or half days) a week.

There is one more alternative. In some large communities, couples or mothers will take a child or two (no more than two) under three or four years of age into their homes under foster day-care plans. To find such a thoroughly qualified foster day-care service, however, it is essential to consult a family, child, or social agency, since these agencies carefully select and supervise the homes. It goes without saying that having the child go through the same gradual transition as described for nursery schools—from mother to substitute mother person—is a must.

If none of these options seems available, or if you know of a good day-care center, the center could be your answer. Day-care centers are sponsored by a variety of different organizations and agencies, including some churches and schools—some with federal funding. A quality day-care center is one based on the concept of "developmental day care," which means the center is not just custodial (a shelter for the child) but is interested in furthering the child's total development. The staff is likely to be warm, accepting, trained in child development, and ready to meet and enrich the physical, emotional, and social needs of the individual child. Caring deeply about children, the staff members (often with para-professionals who are given in-service training) sensitively relate to the youngster, both as teacher and parent substitute. The groups of children are apt to be small, and the ratio of staff to children is adequate. (At best, this ratio should be one adult to five children.) The equipment and program are geared to developing the child's own skills and talents.

So much for the top-rate centers. Unfortunately, these are a drop in the bucket. There are not nearly enough quality day-care centers to go around, and some offer inadequate arrangements that do not serve either the emotional, social, or intellectual needs of the very young child. You also need to watch out for certain privately owned chains of franchised centers (like supermarkets) that are mushrooming all over the country—a booming business for profiteers. They are apt to be understaffed and overcrowded. The bewildered child sees many faces come and go, as sometimes the staff is hired by the hour, to work on a four-hour shift. And, of course, there are other so-called day-care centers that are little more than "custodial parking lots" for young children.

Little by little, however, groups of civic-minded citizens—parents, legislators, child-development experts, and members of women's rights organizations—are pushing for more and better care for children of working parents. It is hoped that gradually more children and mothers will benefit from the very best that day care can offer.

Day Care for the Under-Threes, and Overall Hints

In addition to day care for the child from three to six years of age, there are some infant centers for those under three, many of which are being run as research projects. Much controversy exists regarding the value of day care for such very young children and infants, and the pros and cons are being tested at some of these model projects. In one of the model centers, the youngest group of babies, ranging from two to six months of age, is cared for on a basis of one adult for every two infants, which is rather ideal. In the next group are babies from seven to eleven months, with one adult for every three infants—also quite satisfactory. And in the oldest group, the one- to three-year-olds, one adult is available to every four children—and who can ask for more? Each mother is requested to help her baby make his adjustment to his new surroundings and to become acquainted with the new person or persons who will act as her substitute. During this interim the mother learns much about her own baby as well as about other babies, and she is also helped with any problems she may run into with her infant while at home.

Knowing that primary maternal attachment is the basis for the child's ability to form social attachments later in life, Bettye M. Caldwell, Ph.D., Director of the University of Arkansas

Center for Early Development and Education at Little Rock, says that in an experimental day-care center project in Syracuse that she supervised, all the infants were at least six months old when they were enrolled. "This policy," Dr. Caldwell explains, "was adopted to permit the primary child-mother attachment to develop before the child was placed in a situation that might conceivably weaken it."

Many child-development experts, as well as those who work with children, feel there could be solutions other than day care for the working mother and her child. If industries, businesses, schools, and colleges, etc., could set up nurseries and centers for the very young children of their female employees and staff—who could then visit and play with their children during coffee breaks and lunch, and when the children needed them—the lessening of the mother's tensions and/or guilt feelings would so improve her morale and work performance (to say nothing about her absenteeism) that employer, mother, and child would all benefit.

If you have no other option and are looking for day care for your child, you would want to visit the center you are choosing—first to see how it "feels" to you, carefully observing the children to see if they seem happy and absorbed in interesting activities, and to see whether the children are apparently relating well to one of the adults in charge. Finally, if the center goes along with your desire to let your young child or infant separate from you gradually—as described for the nursery school—this might be just the right "home away from home" for your child.

WHEN PARENTS TAKE VACATIONS

Should We or Should We Not Go?
Even the most conscientious and loving parents of a toddler or baby may have a need for an occasional vacation, a need to get out from under, a chance to take a respite from the constant demands of the very young child and from the inroads he can make on their private lives. Both parents may return home to

their child renewed, relaxed, and refreshed, better equipped to continue their parenting "con amore." Yet there are some parents who feel strongly about not leaving their very young one behind, knowing that both they and the child would feel more secure through being together. This decision, of course, makes for a totally different kind of vacation, but one which may prevent the child from experiencing some temporary difficulties.

Separations of even a few nights can be upsetting to a child during his first two or two and a half years (and for some three-year-olds too). Longer separations can stretch and strain his growing "psychological muscles." The two-year-old is at the stage where he realizes how much Mommy and Daddy mean to him, but he is not yet at the stage where their verbal explanations can mean much to him. Few would deny that a little child is likely to feel distress when both parents leave him—especially his mother, if she has been his chief mainstay. The toddler, so dependent upon his parents, cannot understand the meaning of separation. Is he being punished for doing something wrong? he may wonder. He has no way of knowing he is not going to be left forever.

This sinking feeling of having done something wrong ("What did I do or say that caused him [or her] to leave me?" or "What's wrong with me?") is one of the first thoughts of many an adult when a love affair breaks up. The temporary depressive effect of such a loss may be unconsciously linked with these early fears and/or experiences.

Perhaps all parents feel varying degrees of guilt when they take off. Yet the parent who desperately wants to get away, but feels overwhelmingly guilty and therefore sacrifices the vacation in order to remain with the child, is not going to do himself or herself—or the child—any good, because the youngster may sense the other message, the resentment that goes with the "sacrifice."

The truth remains that no one can tell parents what to *do*.

After they become aware of some of the facts, and examine and weigh them against the particular situation they find themselves in, and consider the sensitivity of their particular

Longer Separations from Parents: Threats to Love

child, they will need to play it by ear and do what *they* believe is best for all.

Nevertheless, there are ways in which you can plan things so that the under-three-year-old (and over) will be able to meet the experience with a minimum of stress. Provided precautionary steps are taken, the child may even gain strength from his experience which may help him to deal more effectively with future stresses and strains. And you can go off with a lighter heart.

Planning for the Child
Regardless of the variables, such as the personality and maturity of the individual child (meaning that one youngster may be more prone to anxiety than another) and the state of his physical and emotional well-being at the time of the separation, here are some of the more practical "iffy" issues:

- If the young child already has a nurse or mother substitute to whom he is attached, naturally the problem is reduced. But if he hasn't someone, *what has been said in earlier chapters needs repetition here:* It is important that the person who comes to stay with the child is someone he already knows and cares for, perhaps a devoted grandparent, relative, favorite sitter or daily housekeeper, who will give him the same kind of consistent care he is used to.
- If this familiar person isn't available and you find a new "someone" who is willing to help you out, be sure she is a warm, reliable person who is good with young children or babies. But let the baby or young child have several days or more to "become accustomed to her face" before you leave so that he will have established a *relationship*, which can mitigate to some extent the pangs of your absence.
- If possible, it is better for your child to remain in his own home rather than being sent elsewhere. Removing him from familiar toys and scenes would again mean burdening him with an additional adjustment. Since continuity signifies so much to a young child, it is prudent to have his routine

followed as usual. However, if he is at an age where he knows Grandma and Grandpa's home, and has already visited there overnight, he may enjoy the stay—as a sort of mini-adventure (provided the stay is a short one)—despite the likelihood of some plaintive questioning: "When are Mommy and Daddy coming back?"

If your child has a younger or older sibling to turn to for companionship, these two babes in the woods will not feel so lost and lonesome. They can give each other moral support and comfort. These are the times when the children, in their need for one another, learn to value the other more, recognizing the brighter side of having a brother or sister. The older one may already have been through a separation and weathered it, knowing that Mommy and Daddy *do* come back. And since a younger sibling usually mirrors the attitudes of the older one, he may be somewhat reassured by his brother or sister's more confident responses. Strangely enough, an older sibling often finds similar relief and support in the company of his younger brother or sister.

Possible Reactions Upon Your Return

Whereas some children do not seem any the worse for the separation, depending upon some of the circumstances described above, for others, a word of caution. Dr. Peter Neubauer suggests that when you return home, do not be surprised if your child gives you a chilly welcome or ignores you while being fairly cordial with his father. He may seem quite angry with you and "act up," which is his manner of declaring he is upset that you went away and hopes you are not going to do *that* again. These actions may be his unconscious way of getting even with you.

What a homecoming! And here you had visualized excited greetings, hugs, and kisses!

Actually, hostile, angry behavior at such a time is a healthy way through which a child can regain his equilibrium. He loves you. He missed you. Maybe he feared you wouldn't return. You are home now and he feels safe enough again to "let it all out."

A fine way of expressing love, you may think. Yet anger

Longer Separations from Parents: Threats to Love

sometimes is a way of restoring love, of clearing the way for the return of positive feelings. It may even show the loved one who has hurt us just how much we love him, that is, if he can ever understand this.

The healthy meaning of aggressive behavior, as shown earlier by Dr. Albert Solnit, is again presented in an example of the behavior of emotionally deprived children. Dr. Solnit tells of young children who have suffered from maternal deprivation in an institution and then are placed in foster homes: ". . . their initial responses of settling in and feeling safe and trusting are frequently followed by aggressive, exploratory, naughty behavior. If the foster parents will continue their steady affectionate care and relationship, these aggressive activities and outbursts will gradually tone down." Dr. Solnit goes on to explain that the child is working toward a *healthy assertiveness,* which can be developed as he finds steady affection. Tragically enough, the evidence of this aggression, Dr. Solnit concludes, "is often perceived by foster parents as evidence of a bad seed or ungrateful behavior, rather than evidence of the return of health, [therefore] these children are often given up by the foster parents at the crucial time. They begin a round of placements and devastatingly traumatic rejections." And soon they give up seeking trust and love in adults.

In contrast to children who act aggressively, there are clingers who become reluctant to let their mothers out of their sights for a while, such as the child who clings excessively to his mother and doesn't want her to leave him at nursery school. This child may be haunted by the fear of his ambivalent feelings toward his mother. At this age—roughly from some time in his third year till about five—the child believes in the magic power of his thoughts and wishes. He may have said (or thought) on occasion, "I hate you! Go away!" Maybe then, he fears, his wishes may come true and his mother *won't* come back. He also may fear that his mother knows how mad he was on certain occasions and might punish him by going away and not coming back.

And then you see the child with a delayed reaction, who will rejoice upon greeting his mother (and father) but then, after a few days, seem apprehensive and anxious, or solemn and quiet.

The provocative behavior, the clinging, the delayed reactions are apt to disappear in due time if you are patient and tolerant, indicating to your child that you are steady in your love despite his (quite normal) reactions and that you have no intentions of going away soon again. And he may need to hear you *say*—even if he cannot fully believe it yet—that you will always return to him. The quality of your day-to-day relationship with your child will help to bring back his confidence and trust in you, and when he is old enough to reason with, he will be able to understand that a trip does not mean desertion.

WHEN PARENTS DIVORCE

Surely no mother or father of very young children arrives at the parting of ways easily. The rift between them undoubtedly was a long time in coming, and by the time the actual divorce took place the children were sensing—in their own ways, according to their ages and sensitivities—that there was trouble between their parents. Dr. Bruno Bettelheim, former Director of the Orthogenic School for chronically disturbed children, University of Chicago, has written, ". . . there is no age at which the child is unaware of, or doesn't respond to what's happening between parents. Some parents assume that if they don't fight in front of their child, he will not be affected, but this just isn't so." According to Dr. Bettelheim, children respond to the emotional *climate* in the home. The child brought up in a serene home (and he surely does not mean to imply this suggests only peace and quiet or no noise or friction between parents, ever) is likely to get a serene outlook on life which may not be noticeable until his maturity. And, if there is *much* discord in the home, the child's insecurity may not show up until much later either.

Therefore, many authorities agree today that if nothing of the marriage can be salvaged, a clean break—painful and hurtful as it is to all at first—is better made earlier than later. Dragging unhappiness, discord, and tension along for years in a marriage can be just as disturbing in other ways to a child, if not more so,

Longer Separations from Parents: Threats to Love

than the present upheaval. Besides, children do need to have a pattern or model of affection and love to follow for their own future lives.

Fortunately, many of today's parents, no matter what their personal bitterness toward each other may be, seem to be more sensitively aware of the importance of setting aside their grievances as they plan together in the best interests of the child. This means they try not to let money matters, education, visitation rights, etc., become battles in which the child is used as a weapon. While they may no longer work together as husband and wife, they may try to work together as parents.

The Infant

Perhaps one could say that a baby is affected by the divorce indirectly more than directly. His total well-being is highly dependent upon his mother's psychological health. That is, if she is depressed or preoccupied with her own difficult readjustments, the problems of rearranging her life—to say nothing about her inner life—she may not be able to supply her infant with the emotional support he now needs. If he is being deprived unwittingly of his basic psychological requirements, he may indicate this deprivation by added crying and fussing and going off his feeding schedules, or even by refusing his food. The baby "feels" his mother's problems too.

At the same time, how can anyone ask or expect a mother who is possibly feeling hurt, angry, and alone to consider only her baby's well-being and to suggest she be warm, loving, and giving as ever?

Should this be your situation, it stands to reason that the easier you can make things for yourself, the easier it will be on your baby. As you face a multitude of problems (and this goes for circumstances including your older children), you may assume you must come to grips with these problems by yourself. You may be under the impression that seeking outside help would be admitting "weakness."

Nothing could be further from the truth.

If you are deeply troubled or just emotionally overburdened, a

The Roots of Love

do-it-yourself approach to your problems doesn't make much sense. Rather, a more courageous and rational step would be to reach out for guidance. Close friends or relatives may be well meaning in their sympathy and "advice," but their point of view is apt to be biased. At such a time, the counsel of someone totally uninvolved with the family would be more expedient. A professionally trained person, specially equipped to deal with just such a family disruption (a counselor at a family or social agency, or a marriage counselor or psychiatrist), may be able to help you clarify some of the issues and complicated emotions that you are grappling with. This help can relieve you personally and leave you freer to turn to your baby—able to give more of yourself to him.

If the baby is past eight months or so, he will surely miss his daddy, to whom he has probably become attached, particularly if this father gave him much time and loving attention. And by the time the toddler has reached ten to eighteen months or thereabouts, his attachment is bound to be even more strongly rooted.

After her father had left home, Lorna, aged fourteen months, would search endlessly under her father's bed and chair and in the closet every morning and evening in the hopes of finding him there again one day. She also whined and cried a lot, which was her way of saying, "I want my daddy! Where is he?" After her father had begun to visit her regularly, she finally made peace with the new arrangements in her life and began to settle down once more.

As in all situations involving separations, whatever can be done to keep the toddler's surroundings the same during and after the divorce will help to reduce the child's anxiety and sense of impending danger. Father's departure in itself was a big enough disruption in continuity for the child. Sensible as it may seem to you at the time, if you send the toddler off to another home (to relatives, friends, whomever), he may get the feeling that he is being deserted by both his parents. And he may despair and grieve. Nevertheless, if he receives an abundance of emotional sustenance from you, during this trying period in *your* own

Longer Separations from Parents: Threats to Love

life, in addition to a good dosage of sameness, you will be giving him the boost he needs to overcome this upset in *his* life.

The Child from Two to Three—and Over

By this time it must be clear to the reader that one of the deepest anxieties of early childhood is the fear of separation from parents. First there is the fear of loss of the parent, then fear of loss of his love, and both together. Separations that have not been carefully handled in early childhood can play havoc with one's love life in adulthood. As stated much earlier, a man or woman may be afraid of love, fearful of being rejected or hurt or abandoned. He or she may be among those who are overly clinging and possessive, overly suspicious and jealous, dependent or demanding, wanting constant "proof" of love.

By understanding that a little child can mourn and grieve in much the same way as an adult when he has lost a loved figure permanently (or temporarily, which for a young child may be perceived of as permanent)—and this can happen to some degree at the time of divorce—you may more readily recognize some of the signs of his distress.

He may deny or repress the fact of his loss ("Daddy will come back to stay with me"), feel guilty, withdraw into himself—losing appetite and *joie de vivre*—and refuse to be consoled. It may take the child some time (during which he may be difficult to handle) to work through his grief and disappointment.

Among the many questions that a toddler between eighteen months and twenty-four months may have in his mind which he cannot ask or even formulate yet is his frightening thought of how he will be able to manage without his daddy. He also may worry that if one parent can vanish so easily, what can keep his other parent from vanishing too? His underlying fear looms up then: Who will take care of *me?*

Words, which may not mean much now, can nevertheless convey *some* reassurance to him, particularly through the sympathetic tone of voice in which these words are spoken. He can be told that Mommy and Daddy are going to live in different houses now, but "Daddy will come to see you a lot." If his father does not renege (and of course a child as young as this will notice the absences), the impact of the disruption of family life on the child may become diluted, and in time he will readjust to the reality of the situation.

Guilts and Fears

As the child moves further into his third year, he can understand more and be told a little more. A three-year-old was able to formulate some of her worries, which she talked about with her nursery school teacher. "Mommy sent Daddy away and 'diforced' him. Maybe if I make her mad she will diforce me too." Under these circumstances a child needs the reassurance that no matter how mad she and her mother are at each other, a mother does not divorce her young children. "Only married people can divorce each other."

Since a young child is not always able to verbalize his questions, it is important—as you tell your child what you feel he is ready to hear—to listen for the tiniest cues as to the questions you believe may bother him, i.e., the questions that lie beneath the questions. Sometimes, as we talk to our children and listen to their silences too, the silence in itself becomes the cue.

Many of today's parents are aware that there comes a time in a little boy's life when he wishes to have Mommy all to himself, and in moments of jealousy, wants his father out of the way. The same goes for a girl's feelings for her father, and her desire at times to have Mommy remove herself as an obstacle. These wishes, and the real events that take place, are usually mixed up in a child's mind at this early age, and the line that separates wishes and deeds is not clearly defined as yet.

Therefore it stands to reason that if a father really does go away from home, the youngster may fear his bad wishes have come true. He may believe on an unconscious level that he is to blame, and, besides feeling guilty, he may fear some kind of retribution. A little girl losing her father through divorce may worry that her mother knew all about her possessive feelings about Daddy and shipped him away to punish her. Or, she may

Longer Separations from Parents: Threats to Love

get the idea that her father left her because he did not love her enough; she didn't quite measure up.

Little girls and boys of this age—and even later—do need help to make them understand they are not to blame in any way for the divorce. No wishes on their part, or actions, such as being naughty, brought on the divorce. Teddy, aged three, solemnly believed his daddy had left him in anger because the evening before he had refused to go to bed on time.

"Both Mommy and Daddy will continue to love and protect you. You are safe," are words they can now understand. Much of the proof of this reassurance depends, naturally, on the contact a father will be willing and able to maintain with his child. If his visits are regular (or if he arranges to have the child or children visit him), the youngster will begin to see that he did not actually "wish Daddy away," that Daddy is still "there" and still loves him. Sometimes, unfortunately, a father repeatedly cancels his promised visits, or makes these visits few and far between. All one can do then is to be honest with the child about the disappointing parent without running that parent down. "Daddy doesn't want to be mean. He doesn't seem to understand how much you love him and how this hurts us all. But we will get along anyhow." This situation is one of those painful realities in life that a child may have to face and learn how to absorb—with some possible residue—but that can be overcome through the steady, sensitive understanding and emotional encouragement the child receives from his other parent and, it is hoped, from relatives.

While a parent may feel justified, it is best not to pin the blame for the divorce on the child's father, or sabotage his image (and the same applies to Father in his relationship to Mother). Youngsters of this or any tender age need and want to believe in *both* parents. They do not want to feel that one of them is "good" and the other "bad." In identifying with his "bad" parent, a child may believe *he* is bad too.

Although the child has thought of Mother and Father together, he will now need to reshape his relationship with his

The Roots of Love

parents and learn to know them again in a different way—as two separate people, but still his mommy and daddy. Many children cling to the fantasy that someday their parents will get together again. The child will have to know from the start that this never can come about. He may want to deny everything you have told him and insist it isn't so. He may cry over the ruptured relationship, and you may have to repeat over and over again that he will be taken care of—always.

You know by now that a crisis in a child's life may bring on all kinds of untoward behavior. He may suck his thumb more frequently, pick at his food, refuse to go to bed at night, or refuse to go to nursery school (if already there), in fear that when he returns home, Mommy will have disappeared too. (The same with difficulties in getting to sleep.) His temper tantrums may be constant instead of intermittent, or his anxiety (and mourning) may show itself by other behavior patterns, which you may not have noticed before or which have become more pronounced.

Although you also know that children of this age are likely to express their feelings through actions (behavior) rather than through words, this behavior may be a constant irritation to you, just one more difficulty for you to cope with. For this reason, you may want to consult with your youngster's pediatrician or nursery-school teacher on how best to help him. Or, you may want to consult another professional as suggested earlier.

Along with seeking this help, you must be aware that the child's behavior symptoms are, like fever, an indication of his need for some kind of special care. Your understanding of this and your ability to comfort him, at a time trying enough for you, may help him believe again that there are loving, faithful people around him who will continue to protect and cherish him.

Life goes on. A child, even as young as two or three, can weather any crisis without suffering permanent damage, provided he receives a fair amount of what has been suggested throughout this chapter. With the passing of time and the child's innate thrust toward health and growth, he will recover from this disruption of his universe. Moreover, as you get a grip on life again, so may he.

 CHAPTER NINE

Healthy Sex Attitudes, Identity, and Development

And now a bird's-eye view of further developments in the psychosexual-social life of the very young child, all of which go a long way in influencing and affecting his later capacity to find fulfillment in his love life. While sexual pleasure for adults can be easily had without love, few would deny that when sex is an expression of, or is accompanied by love, it is one of the deepest and most rewarding of all human experiences.

The child's future capacity to partake in this loving sexuality begins the day he is born. It involves the good feelings he develops about his body and self, the pleasure the boy will derive from being a boy, and the girl from being a girl. Part of this pride in sex identity comes from the cues the baby receives from both parents in their joy that this infant *is* a boy or girl, as well as from the parents' own personal pleasure and satisfaction in being male or female. One may also include the parents' own ability to convey to their child the feeling that his sexual self-explorations and curiosities are normal, and while boys and girls are made differently, they both are whole and equal. In addition, parents contribute to the child's later healthy sexual functioning by allowing him to individuate gradually and become his own person—ideally, a caring human being who can fully love a member of the opposite sex.

Many of us adults have suffered in varying degrees from the attitudes about sex fostered by our parents—attitudes that were really not their "fault" but the fault rather of their times, when there was less available knowledge about sex and little discussion about it. And to go back even further, this "fault" again was also that of our parents' parents, who may have firmly transmitted to *them* the cultural viewpoint of those even earlier times when sex, particularly for girls, was a nonexistent subject, if not thoroughly debased.

But many present-day mothers and fathers who had a hard time of it in their childhoods courageously move ahead to do a better job for their children than was done for them.

Letty Cottin Pogrebin, an editor of *Ms.* magazine, columnist, wife, and mother, states it simply as she reflects about her daughter: "In this second chance at childhood, I hack through a forest of sexual memories to clear a path for you that is not as tangled as my own was."

HOW SEX ATTITUDES DEVELOP

From all the richness and warmth of care your baby received in the earliest days, weeks, and months of life; from all the many things you and his close others did for your baby, he began to learn some important "lessons" about love and sex. As mentioned in the early chapters, by being cuddled and held and fondled, bathed and soothed and changed, your baby gradually began to form a healthy image of his own body.

Genital Self-Discovery: the Boy

Some time during his first year or so, the little baby boy, in learning to use his hands, discovers his mouth, thumb, toes, ears, and maybe finds his penis too. This genital discovery, often occurring during bath time, seems to come about sooner for the boy than for the girl, because, after all, *there it is,* visible and accessible. The discovery may bring with it a vague sensuous pleasure, since even at this early age the penis is far more sensitive than the baby's other extremities. Unfortunately, some parents (and many grandparents) take Baby's delighted reaction to be a sure sign that their baby boy is well on his way to sexual precocity and preoccupation. In the past, less so today, many parents would declare "Don't touch!" or pull the baby's hand away or distract the infant or frown. But we now know that these responses may further increase the baby's interest in this particular section of his anatomy. Or, the baby can get the notion that there is something bad or wrong with this part of himself—a notion that can seriously affect his sexual attitudes.

Genital pleasure, even now with mild arousal (which becomes sporadic masturbation as the child becomes a little older), is only part of the child's total life and development. Babies raised in institutions who receive only minimal amounts of affectionate care and stimulation find pleasure in self-stimulation their only source of body comfort and satisfaction, so they may go at it a good part of the day (although some others may either lose all interest in their own bodies or fail to develop this vital interest). But with the normally raised child, genital pleasure is just one small portion of the many pleasures he experiences.

A little boy may have erections even during his first year—also quite normal—and these may appear before or after urinating, after being changed and cleaned and dried, or when he has touched his penis. An enlightened mother and father in today's world may want to tell their baby approvingly, "Yes, this is your penis," especially if the baby points to it.

Genital Self-Discovery: the Girl
The girl baby may come upon her genitals somewhat later, as explained above, often in her second year (yet occasionally sooner than this). Sometimes the little girl will poke around and find her navel, then her clitoris, and, much later, her vagina. Dr. James A. Kleeman, Associate Professor of Psychiatry, Yale Medical School, has observed that the little girl around this age is apt to show a good deal of pride and pleasure in her body, "including her external genital area." Dr. Kleeman points out that she may also become intrigued by all the "holes" in her body: navel, ears, eyes, mouth, etc.

Although a two-year-old may be a little young for a long lecture on anatomy, if the child asks you then, or later (which may be more likely), or looks up at you questioningly while exploring her genitals, she may need a simple answer. In the past, parents were apt to speak of "your privates" or "your private parts," which of course cast a veil of secrecy over this area. Yet a good many of us still find it awkward and somewhat difficult to explain, even when the child is a bit older and wants to know the names of things: "Yes, Betty, that is your clitoris." No matter. If you feel more at ease using family terms, those individual household nicknames, by all means use them. (It has been found that mothers are more prone to embarrassment in naming their girls' genitals than in naming their boys'.) But if, in time, you can get used to the correct terminology—and you will have plenty of opportunities to repeat these words—you will find that both you and your child will be better able to accept these words and mention them less self-consciously. More important than the use of words is the accepting tone that goes along with the explanations, as well as an accepting understanding of the young child's normal fascination with her body.

Masturbation

The girl, as well as the boy, discovers pleasurable genital sensations as she touches herself—and who isn't inclined to repeat pleasurable experiences? Later on, masturbation is one form of solace that a child may turn to when he or she is tired, upset, or tense; but sometimes when parents see a child clutch at his or her genitals, they take it to be masturbation when it just may be a need to go to the toilet, or, especially with the little boy who clutches his penis, an expression of tension or fear.

Even though we know that masturbation is not a "wrong" thing, cannot physically harm a child, and that most everyone masturbates at some time or times in his or her life as child and adult, the word itself makes some of us uncomfortable, and we feel uneasy at finding our child thus occupied. Obviously, we cannot toss aside all at once our own emotions, our past guilts and upbringing, but we can try to detach ourselves somewhat from our feelings and avoid interfering or saying "Stop that!" Many children, however, do seem to learn early—perhaps through observation, perhaps through being told—that one does not masturbate publicly. Naturally, should a child be constantly preoccupied with genital arousal, it would indicate that probably something was missing in his daily life—other stimulation or opportunities for self-expression—or that the child has emotional tensions or difficulties and is in need of some professional help.

Discovery of Sex Differences: the Boy

Up to the time he sees a little girl or his mother naked or using the toilet, a boy usually believes that all people, big or little, are made just as he is made. Unless the boy has been prepared somehow for the revelation that girls and women are penisless, he may just deny the fact to himself, or try to find out for himself this is not so. (Some boys who are not helped to understand about sex differences continue to "try to find out" after they are past three or four by prying under the dresses of little girls, or through other exploratory sex behavior with them.)

The little boy is apt to wonder whether the girl was physically injured in some way. Maybe "it" was taken away from her because she touched it too. It's rather scary for him to think, even unconsciously, "If I'm not careful, something may also happen to mine." "Castration anxiety," fear of injury to one's genitals, is one of mankind's universal although subconscious fears. Much can be done at this age to keep this fear from becoming a problem to the child later on.

Around the time when the little boy is learning to regulate his bowels and bladder, he sometimes fears his penis may be flushed down the toilet (after all, feces is part of him, too, and can be lost easily). Consequently, he may refuse to have anything to do with the toilet for a while, but not know just why. Some little boys may suddenly balk at having a haircut, or they may draw back from touching a broken toy, or they may grab their penis at times to assure themselves it is still there. These and other seemingly odd reactions around two and three may be related to the little boy's sense of the fragility and vulnerability of his body, particularly his penis.

Strangely enough, even in this sexually permissive day, ancient admonitions still persist. The mother of one three-year-old could

The Roots of Love

not understand why her boy refused to hold his penis while urinating, but soon discovered that a housekeeper had warned him, "If you touch it, it will fall off." (There are some other unconscious fears connected with the child's worry about his body integrity that have to do with another happening in his inner life, and these will be discussed shortly.)

The most you can do is to reassure your little boy that a boy cannot lose his penis, that nothing is likely to change it or happen to it. He will want to know that little girls are built in one way from the very start, like their mommies, and boys are built in another way, like their daddies. Most of all he will want to know that his parents are proud he is a boy. Perhaps, in trying to convince himself that all was well, a young three-year-old boy went around announcing to all and sundry, "Do you know that boys have penises and girls have vaginas?" Another boy, at nursery school, also uncertain about male and female differences, made a "widdler" out of putty and pressed it into the doll with which he was playing.

In the process of defining his identity, a little boy may express his desire to "grow a baby too," and be disappointed when he is told it isn't possible. But he can be somewhat reconciled to hear that while little girls when they are grownup can grow babies inside of them, give birth to the babies, feed and bathe them, and put them to bed, a boy when he is grownup can help to *make* a baby, and he too can give the baby a bottle, bathe it, and put it to bed. (You could add that he will find out how he can help to make a baby when he is just a little older. He is not likely to ask *now*, but when you feel he is ready, there is a delightful book* which, as you read it to him, will explain these facts.)

A little boy first identifies with his mother, his primary love. He wants to be like her and do what she does. Gradually, he makes the transition to an identification with his father (or some substitute male figure if his father is absent or deceased), which helps him to consolidate his sense of being a male. (During doll-play or with miniature "people" in housekeeping play, a

---

* *The Wonderful Story of How You Were Born* by Sidonie Matsner Gruenberg. Doubleday and Co., Inc., Garden City, New York, revised edition, 1970.

Healthy Sex Attitudes, Identity and Development

child of either sex plays out some of his inner confusions, conflicts, and fantasies—some of them sexual. The child may reenact part of his daily life with his family as he sees it or interprets it—or would like it to be. This kind of play serves as a safety valve through which he may work out and master some of his deeper anxieties. By watching and listening to your youngster's doll-play you may pick up some remarkable clues as to how he views you!)

Interestingly enough, since time immemorial, both men and women have shown envy of each other's sex functions and roles. Mythology is full of allusions to man's envy of woman's ability to procreate. Take the god Zeus for example. Annoyed and exasperated by his pregnant wife's wisdom, he swallowed her up and eventually delivered the goddess Athena through his forehead. One version of the Dionysius myth describes Zeus tearing the six-month-old fetus from the burning body of his mortal love Semele, sewing it up into his loins, and carrying it to full term, thereby giving birth to Dionysius. A California psychoanalyst, Dr. Lawrence J. Friedman, brings this theme down to earth as he observes that man's daily language is laced with expressions such as "This is my creation, my baby." Or, he suggests, "One can be pregnant with a new idea, give birth to, have an abortive thought, have a brain child, etc." Besides, in different parts of the world, particularly in some primitive societies, a ritual existed (and may still exist in certain cultures) known as "couvade," in which a husband would take to bed at the time of his wife's confinement and go through all the motions of labor. He would moan and groan and thresh about while his wife quietly gave birth. Family and friends paid homage and brought gifts to *him!* And many modern men experience "pregnancy symptoms" (temporary weight gains, insomnia, nausea) or "sympathy pains" (backaches, headaches, indigestion, cramps, etc.) during their wives' pregnancies and at the time of birth.

No man has only male characteristics or "traits," as no woman has only female ones. In varying degrees our personalities are admixtures of, and are enriched by, qualities we acquire from both our parents.

The Roots of Love
Discovery of Sex Differences: the Girl
Depending on whether the toddler under three (sometimes later than this) already has been informed about the sexual distinction between girl and boy, or has seen her father or older or younger brother naked, or has been to the toilet with a playmate of the opposite sex, or observed statues, pictures or household pets, one day she notices there is a difference between male and female genitals. Now, the under-threes and over seem never to have heard about the Women's Lib stance on penis envy! As you listen to and watch youngsters of this age, at toilet time in particular (and just spend a few mornings observing at a nursery school, or talk to a nursery-school teacher), you may notice that quite a few of them are confused and curious about the sex organs and functions of the opposite sex. Initially, a little girl is apt to display, overtly or covertly, varying degrees of disappointment and anxiety when she first discovers that a distinct part of her body seems to be missing.

In the typically egocentric way of thinking at this age, the little girl, just as the little boy, may be shaken as she discovers all people are not made as she is.

Proud as Mary may have been up to now about her body, she, like all children who want to have what the other child has, wants a penis too. It's much fancier, she may think about the male appendage, and it's so nice to wee-wee with. (And many little girls will attempt to urinate like boys.) She may then be somewhat annoyed with her mother, who "borned me without a peenie," as one little three-year-old lamented to her father. She also may worry that her penis was taken away because she was "bad" or had touched it. But she still may entertain hopes of growing one soon. One youngster, aged three, with two older brothers, who felt shortchanged bodily, begged her father, "Daddy, please buy me a penuss for Christmas!"

There is no need to make a federal case out of this issue, but it still might be helpful to take a look at the Victorian era, when Freud first startled the world with his statements about "penis envy."

As we can see it now, women in those days certainly were

Healthy Sex Attitudes, Identity and Development

second-class citizens. They were subjugated and demeaned, and had little of life besides *kinde, küche und kirche* (children, kitchen and church). They were not supposed to enjoy sex—certainly not "good" women and wives. The little girl's discovery of her body lack—as she felt it then, since no one helped to enlighten her as to the wholeness, completeness, and loveliness of her body, or to enjoy her femaleness and worth as a person—made her see the penis as a symbol of male strength and power and competence, which, naturally, she also wanted. (All of this is, of course, an oversimplification and just a capsule version of a far more complex psychic phenomenon than is here described.) But today's little girls are certainly more fortunate than their Victorian ancestors.

Virginia or Mabel or Mary needs to be told and shown in countless ways that being a girl is wonderful; that little girls and their mommies are built in one way and boys and their daddies in another way—and each way is right for them. You might want to add that no girl ever had a penis or lost it, nor will she ever grow one.

It may take quite a while for the little girl to accept these facts, since, as said earlier, very young children have a stubborn way of clinging to their own fantasies, horrendous as they may be. Yet a parent can lead a child gradually to a recognition of the realities of life.

The little girl of three or so may be reassured to know that when she becomes a grown woman, she can, if she wants to, grow babies inside her just as Mommy did, and that she will develop breasts like Mommy to feed her baby with. She will surely get to feel she is wanted and cherished by her parents for being a girl, through their attitudes toward her, through her mother's self-esteem as a woman, a person, and a mother.

In her autobiography *Blackberry Winter: My Earlier Years*, Margaret Mead writes to this point:

> I was always glad that I was a girl. I cannot ever remember wanting to be a boy. It seems to me this was because of the way I was treated by my parents. I was a wanted child and when I was

born I was the kind of child my parents wanted. This sense of satisfying one's parents probably has a great deal to do with one's capacity to accept oneself as a kind of person.

It is around this time or even earlier that the little girl begins to find Daddy pretty special in a new way—and more about this later.

Birth Fantasies of Young Children

Should you ask your nearly threes and over how and where they think babies come out of their mommies' bodies (if they already know that Mommy grows babies inside her), do not be surprised if you hear the most utterly extravagant and preposterous imaginings ever. And do bear in mind that, whatever you say, your firsthand information may be inwardly scorned and rejected by the child, although politely listened to, and your young one will need firm repetition of answers to questions which he may ask you over and over again. He needs time to digest the information, so the less information he is given at one time, the better. (Remember, he or she may have no intentions of becoming an obstetrician!)

Dr. Kleeman, who has made in-depth studies on how core gender identity (which we will come to later) is solidly established in girls by age three, writes of a very normal, curious little girl, Matti, whom he observed over a period of years. Matti at this time is twenty-two and a half months old, and a brother has just been born. Matti's mother has already briefed her daughter about her pregnancy and about Matti's own body—facts easily put to the child as she was undressing her doll, Betty. Dr. Kleeman uses his material to illustrate a number of other points, including some of the ways in which gender identity is established. But here, a vignette from "The Establishing of Core Gender Identity in Normal Girls" is used to point out some of the confusions little girls have about exactly "where" the newborn emerges:

> MATTI: "Betty be born. Betty be born from Matti's belly. Matti go away. Mommy stay home. Betty be born, doctor help . . ."

Healthy Sex Attitudes, Identity and Development

MOTHER: "Oh really, Matti, how did Betty get out of Matti's belly?"
MATTI (with confidence): "Out of a special hole."
MOTHER: "Oh really?"
MATTI: "Not out of Matti's BM tushy, out of special hole."
Matti with gesture and words points to several places: to her "belly button," breast, genitals. She is vague but not upset by her unsureness. She said, "Big hole Mommy."
MATTI (again vaguely): "Big hole, little hole . . ."

Do not be surprised if your child asks you questions (a) when you are in a hurry to go out, (b) while you are on a bus with an armful of packages, or (c) while you are waiting at the checkout counter at the supermarket; or when he tells you in front of strangers or guests that "Mommy eats something, then grows a baby and it comes out the BM place." Yet this inspired fantasy does have its logic, since up to now the youngster has known his anatomy mostly in terms of eating and eliminating.

It is worth helping the child save face and dignity when he makes such remarks by trying not to laugh (easier said than done), but rather attempting something like this: "Many children think as you do, but it is this way . . ." It also may be wise to first put some questions to the child, as Matti's mother did, before you give him the real facts so he can clear out some of the cobwebs that have collected in his fantasy life. When these cobwebs are gradually pushed aside, room will be made in the child's mind to accept the real explanations. (Freud once spoke of not putting new wine into old bottles.)

If your throat seems to go dry, if you seem tongue-tied or stammer as you first try to explain some of the "facts," feel reassured that your fellow sisters and brothers are legion. No matter what we *know*, those old taboos about sex from the past sometimes pop up at moments like this to inhibit us. Besides, we often find we cannot discuss matters about birth and sex as easily and nonchalantly as we can discuss the season's fashions or the latest books. But then, the questions of birth and love and sex do involve some of our deepest and most intimate feelings—emotions that are far beyond our children's comprehension. Perhaps it isn't all that bad for our children to infer from our manner that we do care deeply about these issues. At any rate, it really does not matter so much *what* you say, or even *how* you say it, as long as you are willing to help him along with his queries. What is important is the feeling you are beginning to get across to your child: that you will always take his questions seriously, that he will not be brushed off. (And he'll start to wonder if and why you don't come back to those unanswered questions raised at the bus, supermarket, etc.) In this way, a child begins to learn that it is all right to ask anything about sex, just as it is all right to find out all about the other exciting things in the world.

SEX IDENTITY AND SEX ROLES

Besides the discovery of his or her own genitals, and the realization that there are differences in the appearance and functions of boy and girl genitals, there are a number of other ways in which a little boy or girl becomes certain of his or her gender by the time the child is three years of age, or younger. Some authorities now believe this gender awareness is already well formed in the latter part of the second year, and is even noticeable by the end of the first year.

To avoid confusion, it might be helpful to explain that *core gender identity* is the young child's inner feeling that he or she belongs to one sex rather than the other. *Gender role identity* is the child's feeling that he is behaving according to the cultural standards of how a boy or girl *should* behave or act.

Is this basic identity learned psychologically, or socially, or is there some inner programming that tells the child he is a he or she is a she? Are there special male and female characteristics and behavior? Are these learned or are they inherent?

Such controversial issues puzzle many modern parents, and some experts too. There are those who worry that unisex clothes and jobs will seriously interfere with a child's capacity to identify himself and others as a male or female, while others want to do all they can to prevent their children from being trapped into rigidly set male or female stereotypes. Some, like Professor

Healthy Sex Attitudes, Identity and Development

Higgins in *My Fair Lady*, wish that a woman were more like a man, while others cry out "Vive la difference!"

At our present state of knowledge, the most that can be done here is to try to sort out some of the current thinking and a few of the issues, which may well be "emotional land mines"!

Generally speaking, we do know that hormonal, biological, psychological, and cultural differences all contribute to the uniqueness of male and female. Parents who have had both a girl and boy baby notice sooner or later how differently they are built, and how different is their body language. A boy's frame and structure point to wider shoulders, a greater distribution of muscle, whereas a girl may have more fatty tissue and slightly wider hips. The boy, usually bigger, more solid and stronger, is well equipped for heaving and throwing. It is a fairly well accepted fact that male hormones, androgens, contribute to the male's greater *capacity* for aggressive behavior, as well as to his vigor and activity. Many little boys, as we shall see, show these tendencies in their play. But Drs. John Money, Professor of Medical Psychology and Pediatrics at Johns Hopkins Hospital, and Anke A. Ehrhardt, Assistant Professor of Research, Departments of Pediatrics and Psychiatry at the State University of New York, have found that improper functioning of the adrenal glands in the female fetus can, among other possible influences, produce an excess of the androgen hormone, which has a "masculinizing effect on the fetal brain" in girls, thereby causing *extreme* tomboyism later.

Dr. Kleeman believes not only that girls and boys are different, but that what they learn is different. He is also of the opinion that these "learning experiences are sufficiently powerful to make them the predominant forces in determining core gender identity." And there is some good evidence.

Dr. Money and associates at Johns Hopkins Hospital made studies some years ago on large numbers of intersexed individuals: hermaphrodites and pseudohermaphrodites. These are persons whose external sex organs do not match (to varying degrees) their internal sex organs, chromosomes, and hormones—some having external organs of both sexes. They found, among the majority of such individuals, the following facts: If the parents and doctor assigned a sex—let us say male—at birth or shortly thereafter, and this child was reared as a boy by his parents, he would see himself unshakably as a boy by the age of two and a half or so, regardless of the appearance of the outer genitals. This extraordinary finding has also been substantiated by Dr. Robert J. Stoller, Professor of Psychiatry at the University of California at Los Angeles Medical Center. In his words, "even boys without penises do not doubt they are males if their parents also believe this without question. Such a defect may cause problems in the later development of their masculinity, yet they take for granted that they are males."

Although this evidence has been drawn from observations on children with sexual anomalies, many authorities agree today that the determining influences on a child's basic sense of gender identity are those psychic messages that are flashed between parents and child: the attitudes parents reveal to their child about his particular sex.

When a baby is born, we immediately start to program the infant in our minds, first perhaps in terms of pink for the girl or blue for the boy, and we choose, more often than not, distinctly male or female first names. Without our even knowing this, we send out a barrage of messages that are quite different for our boys versus our girls.

Do Little Boys and Girls Play with the Same Toys?

Parents often wonder whether they should offer their under-three-year-old girls "boy toys"—trucks, trains, etc.—rather than dolls, doll equipment, furniture and tea sets (although how many little girls see their Mommies pour tea at home out of tea sets these days?), and whether girls would be just as happy with the more active toys. Some parents feel toys should become desexed altogether, and that advertisements should show girls and boys playing with all the variety of toys available.

To determine whether or not girls and boys of about a year or so would play differently and with different toys if they were put into a free-play situation, researchers Susan Goldberg, of the

Healthy Sex Attitudes, Identity and Development

University of Zambia, and Michael Lewis, of Educational Testing Service, observed thirty-two girls and thirty-two boys aged thirteen months at the Fels Research Institute. While there seemed to be no significant difference in the overall toy preferences, there were significant differences in both time spent with the individual toys and the ways in which they were used. The girls more often chose toys that involved the use of fine muscle coordination (peg boards, blocks, etc.), while the boys—using larger muscles—would run around the room with the toys, banging them and utilizing them more vigorously. As an example, they would often take the "lawnmower" and roll it over the other toys. Furthermore, the little boys spent a lot of time with nontoys, examining doorknobs, lights, covered outlets, etc. The girls tended to sit and play more quietly with a combination of toys, and they seemed to be more dependent upon their mothers than were the boys.

Nevertheless, it is hard to tell whether the dependency was innate or not, because the researchers noted that the mothers had already been relating differently to their girls than to their boys since the children were six months old, vocalizing more with their girl babies than with their boy babies. Other studies also have shown that parents seem to touch and handle female babies more than males, allowing the boys more freedom and autonomy but keeping the girls more dependent upon them.

But here, Dr. Jerome Kagan, Harvard University psychologist, has a word to say about a girl baby's greater dependency. In a fascinating interview with Cynthia Lang for *Parents'* magazine, Dr. Kagan shows how much faster the infant girl develops during the first twelve months—particularly in her intellectual development. He says the girl's precocious growth has to do with "myelinization," the growth of a fatty sheath around nerve fibers, which proceeds faster in girls than in boys. Dr. Kagan writes, "Hence the girl is physically a more mature organism." He goes on to say:

> Since the major cause of fear in the first year of life is exposure to unfamiliar events, then the more acute your awareness of the

world, the more vulnerable you will be to fear. In a sense, the price of the girl's advancement may be more frequent fear. If you put boys and girls in an unfamiliar room, the girls will be likely to show anxiety and cling to their mothers. The boys on the other hand, not realizing that the situation is strange, don't become anxious.

Therefore, according to this view, part of what seems to be more dependent and passive behavior in little girls may well be a sign of advanced development!

Recently, many children's books have been under fire for depicting girls as timid, passive, fearful, intellectually dull, while boys are just the reverse. A number of these books also have been attacked for portraying mommies—even animal mommies—primarily in the kitchen, baking cookies and pies, and always wearing aprons. To be sure, why shouldn't Mommy *also* be drawn wearing a lab coat, a medical jacket, artist's smock, or be shown working at her desk, talking on the telephone—or even reading a book? Wouldn't these pictures then give little girls and boys the idea that there could be other activities in the home (or out of the home) than *only* domestic ones?

Many child-care experts seem to agree that little girls should be given an opportunity to play with cars and trucks, if they want to, and that little boys should have an equal opportunity to nurture by playing freely with dolls. They also would agree that a child can be shown through picture books that there are different kinds of mommies (and daddies, too, some of whom also feed the baby and work together in the home with Mommy), and that a little girl's life can have the fun, excitement, and adventure usually reserved for a boy. However, they also feel that nothing should be *imposed* or *forced* upon the child. And they see the little girl's delight in playing with the so-called "feminine" toys and housekeeping corner (at home, nursery school, or day-care center) as having to do with the girl's desire to identify with her mother's early nurturing role. (One mother was cheered to see her little two-and-a-half-year-old daughter playing with her brother's fire engine, until she noticed the child was using the engine as a crib into which she tucked her doll!)

Healthy Sex Attitudes, Identity and Development
How Children Tell the Difference Between Adult Males and Females

Even at six months, the little girl baby may be more coy and charming with her father than with her mother, Dr. Kleeman observes. He describes the behavior of the girl at about nine months:

> The little girl of 9 months behaves differently with mother and father. For example, if father is present at bath-time she may show much more splashing and attention-seeking activity than when mother is there. She may also be selectively flirtatious and seductive with her father by this age. By 1 year the capacity to differentiate mother from father is often extensive. The flirting, coyness, contact with glances, seeking-kisses behavior with her father and not with her mother may be striking—so that the girlishness of the child's behavior (as defined by the culture) can be very clear-cut at 1, leaving little doubt in the eyes of the stranger that this is a little girl and not a little boy.

At fifteen months or thereabouts, a toddler may look at pictures of boys and girls and make the sex distinction—even though boys and girls pictured are fully clothed. Soon the toddler can perceive the difference between man and woman. The differences noticeable to the young observer show up in the varied clothes worn by men and women and in the way they wear their hair—longish hair on men and unisex clothes notwithstanding—since contours in those clothes differ, as in the female and male body build, carriage, etc. Besides the pictures, in real life the facial appearance and expression, the voice, gestures, texture of skin, and muscle tone all are perceived and distinguished as male or female by the little child.

Sex Role Identity

Even after the little boy has acquired a good sense of his maleness, he will feel more secure if he does not get the impression that he is deviating too far from what is called "sex role standards." This is the child's own yardstick for measuring how well he fits into the cultural image of what is male, and

The Roots of Love

which affects his sense of gender role identity. It is here that parents can help to change some of the harmful and stifling sex typing that has been set up for little girls and boys. We know boys are usually discouraged from showing emotion and tenderness in our culture (see chapter 3), and it takes a very strong man, strong in his sense of maleness, to be able to display such emotions. Little boys are often reminded, "Don't be a sissy." "Keep a stiff upper lip." "Boys don't cry." (Yet we know that in some European, Far Eastern, and Latin American countries, men will cry freely.) Little girls are also prompted often enough that "Girls should act like little ladies, not like tomboys." "Girls don't sit that way." "Girls don't get their clothes dirty."

It might be advantageous for all if we could bury some of the false standards that are still being imposed on our young. Talents, interests, feelings don't come in gender (although we would have good reason to worry if our boys still preferred to play exclusively with dolls, or play at being Mother, past the age of five or six). In permitting children to have access to all kinds of toys, feelings, and experiences, we help them to develop into flexible adults. Parents can try, along with other parents, to keep their children's personalities from becoming hemmed in—even imprisoned—by this outmoded sex stereotyping. We might then be helping our children to experience greater freedom and capacity for self-expression, and, as they grow up, to develop more sensitivity to, and mutual understanding of, each other's needs as man and woman.

Whether he is a poet, businessman, artist, or sportsman, whether he likes to arrange flowers or not, cook (not just steaks outdoors!) or not, diaper and feed his baby, or prefer to give a hand around the house in *other* ways in sharing domestic responsibilities, the father who loves his boy and shows it by keeping up a warm, affectionate relationship with him is likely to raise a son who will develop a firm sense of his maleness.

The same goes for the little girl. A mother who enjoys being a female and accepts her own sexual role—and she may be a policewoman, accountant, ballet dancer, or store executive, or she may not work outside the home—will surely transmit to her

Healthy Sex Attitudes, Identity and Development

daughter the satisfactions of being a woman and an individual. Beyond this, a father's pleasure in having a daughter, and his special relationship with her, contribute to her healthy sex development as a woman, and to the prevention of sexual difficulties later on.

A child's sense of his (or her) sex identity is vital to his total sense of who he is as an individual, and his sense of being an individual contributes to his sex identity.

HEALTHY SEX DEVELOPMENT

"Oedipus" is hardly news today, but its implications need some recapitulation here. In the ancient Greek myth, King Oedipus fulfilled an ancient prophecy by unwittingly killing his father and then marrying his mother. Freud used this myth and Sophocles's drama about it (in addition to his self-analysis and the analysis of patients) to describe what is called the "Oedipus complex," which has to do with the child's intense, erotic attachment to the parent of the opposite sex. This special, possessive kind of attachment begins at some time during the child's third year, or maybe later, and ends usually by the time he (or she) is past five or six. The Oedipal drama—sometimes called "The Family Romance"—is particularly apparent in the small, closely knit family in our Western society. It brings in its wake some mighty powerful emotions of love, hate, jealousy, fear, and guilt, emotions that seem all out of proportion to the size of the children's tiny bodies. For part of the child's painful conflicts are (in a boy) his feelings of resentment and antagonism toward the same-sexed parent, whom he dearly loves but who stands in his way to an "exclusive" on mother. He also believes that if he feels angry with his father, his father will echo this feeling and retaliate and punish him.

Some parents may think, "What nonsense! Our Johnny or Mary never showed any such signs of attachment!"

We need to realize that the emotions children grapple with are primarily on an unconscious level, and the child is not really aware of either his strivings or of his conflicts. This dramatic interlude in the child's sexual growing up is not often acted out in his daily life—although it may be revealed subtly through his play, or even through words. Besides, we also know that our assorted variety of children express and meet their problems in a variety of ways. One forthright young man, aged three years and two months, announced to his father at breakfast one morning, "When I grow up, I'm going to marry Mommy and have babies with her!" His father, although amused, concealed his amusement and quietly tried to straighten things out in his son's mind. "Sorry, Billy, but Mommy is married to me. When you grow up, you can find someone *like* Mommy and marry her." Another single-minded little girl who wanted her father's exclusive attention said to her mother impatiently, "Go away, Mommy! Can't you see I am talking to Daddy?" Some children go so far as to be openly seductive to the object of their love. As one mother described it to a friend, "Tony is so 'Oedipal' these days. He wants to crawl all over me and hug me every chance he can get." Some will provoke their same-sexed parent, who may wonder, "What has gotten into Beth these days? She's so 'ornery'!" Others, especially those whose words and feelings are not so easily expressed, may have more than their usual quota of tantrums and nightmares.

It goes without saying that all these different kinds of strange, ardent, or seemingly uncalled-for behaviors may be the weather vane that tells you your child is having a rough time with his inner struggles.

Fortunately, if all goes well, by the time the child reaches five or six—way beyond the scope of this book—he will emerge from these present clouds of conflict and confusion. He will relinquish "The Impossible Dream" and will find his true place in the family. He will learn to love both of his parents, not in fantasy, but in a more realistic, down-to-earth way. He will realize he is his father's son, not his rival, and his mother's son, not her lover. The same—more or less—happens with the girl in relation to her father. When the child discovers that his parents do not go along with his romantic feelings, do not share them, but think and feel differently, he *begins* to lose some of his egocentric way of

Healthy Sex Attitudes, Identity and Development

thinking. Now he wants to please his parents, and not only be pleased by them. The Oedipal drama will have been successfully brought to a partial conclusion, and at this time the child will have laid down to an even greater extent an emotionally healthy foundation for his or her later functioning in love as a male or female. Dr. Theodore Lidz expresses it quite cogently: "He has found peace with both parents by repressing the erotic aspect of his attachment to one. Nevertheless the erotic attachment survives in the unconscious and will become a determinant of later relationships . . ."

There is a mild reawakening of these feelings in adolescence, when the young person has a second chance to free himself from whatever is left of his childhood attraction to Mom (or Dad, for the girl), and move on to more adult relationships with them and with his own peers.

And now for a brief but closer took at the Oedipal boy and girl and their conflicts.

The Boy and His Parents

As we have seen, children around three are apt to have a belief in the magic power of their wishes. They are sure that what they *think* will come true. Only *part* of Johnny wants his rival to disappear. If his wishes came true, he'd lose his father, whom he loves. He is happy when Daddy is there to give him a knowing look, a smile, an affectionate pat, or a bear hug. With the same kind of magic thinking, Johnny may worry that Daddy can read his mind—the worst part, of course. Since there are also some erotic and sexual components in the little boy's love for his mother, the child may have unconscious fears that his father may punish him for having these sexual sensations. This gives him an added reason for being concerned (as mentioned earlier) for the safety of his genitals: the castration fears. Such ideas are so frightening that they are pushed even further into his unconscious. Yet, along with the strength of his love for his father, these very fears—if not reinforced by the presence of a threatening, harsh male parent—motivate him toward a positive resolution of his dilemma (even though the fears may continue for a while and

The Roots of Love

reappear in disguise, i.e., those animals and monsters that chase and threaten him in his nightmares).

Can parents do anything to help? They can, in many indirect ways. But the most important and meaningful part of their work was done long ago. It is now believed that the good and loving relationships the infant and toddler had with his parents preceding this time in his development is the best "shot in the arm" to help him get through his present difficulties healthily.

More than this, some understanding of what his or her young boy's problems may be about is apt to prevent a parent from being shocked by his child's behavior, treating him too severely or shaming or teasing him about his feelings should he express them. Parents are still parents to their child, and husband and wife to each other. A mother still can be affectionate and hug her little boy, as any mother will who loves her child. She also can gently encourage his growing independence and show her pride as he masters each step away from her. Should the boy want to sleep in Daddy's bed when his father is away, or should he want to come into his parents' bed at night, he can be told, with compassion as well as firmness, that household rules for him and for Daddy are not the same. This does not mean that Sunday-morning romps and bed snuggles are taboo—although it is discreet to be on guard for too much excitement that can have sexual undertones.

A father and mother can help their boy to see that, yes, they *do* share a special private life, special feelings, and a special relationship together that has nothing to do with him and from which he must be excluded. Yet he needs to understand that they also have a different kind of special loving relation with him.

With this help—again, quite some time after the ages covered in this book—the child's anxieties gradually diminish and he turns his energies outward, toward learning, toward the world outside of his home and parents. He decides to emulate his father and try to become the kind of child his father will respect. Someday then, he hopes, he'll find his own wife, who will admire and love him as his father is admired and loved by his mother. His sense of maleness is now becoming even more foolproof.

Healthy Sex Attitudes, Identity and Development

Unfortunately, things do not always work out so smoothly. In some cases, an unhappy mother, disappointed in her husband, may step right onto the stage of her son's drama. Often without being aware of it, flattered by her son's attachment to her, she turns to him for most of her compensations and satisfactions. She then may try to bind him too closely to her, which makes it more difficult for him, if not impossible, to resolve the Oedipus complex. Should this occur, he may have problems later in relating to women—even suffer the crippling of his capacity to enjoy heterosexual relationships. Unless, of course, the boy's father manages to offset his mother's all-enveloping hold through continuing a warm, steady, and firm relationship with his boy.

Now this certainly does not mean to imply that a mother shouldn't feel flattered by her young son's feelings for her. It is warming to know you are so much needed and wanted. A sensitive mother will not want to reject her little son's loving overtures, and can comfortably continue to give him the affection he wants without stimulating his sexuality.

The Girl and Her Parents

The under- (or over-) three-year-old girl faces a slightly different situation. As she moves further away psychically from her mother in the process of separation-individuation, she finds a new love object to adore: her father. Naturally, she would like to displace her mother and have this rival disappear (just as with the little boy in relation to his father). But if Mommy *did* go away, what would little Lolita do? She still needs and loves her mother, who is the very source of her comfort, well-being, daily care, and affection. Even if Mommy works outside the home, the little girl may "remember" how close she was to her as an infant, and how happy she is to be with her at the end of the day. Furthermore, maybe Mother knows what her naughty thoughts are—especially her vague wish to have Daddy be the father of her babies. Maybe then Mommy would stop loving her altogether.

As with the little boy, the girl child has to work her way through this family triangle and find her proper place in the

The Roots of Love

home. But for the "duration," Mother may find it rough going with a little daughter who is affectionate and loving at one moment and altogether exasperating in the next. Usually a mother and father do get across the feeling to their daughter, without deriding her or increasing her sense of guilt, that her hopes are unattainable. Father admires and loves his daughter as always, and shows his affection as ever—without responding to her romancing. She is not "Daddy's little woman," but rather "Daddy's little girl." In time, around five or so, the child becomes aware that her father and mother belong to each other in a certain way and that she cannot disrupt this partnership. Her guilt feelings in relations to her mother tend to diminish, but before she has made peace with her conflicts, she too may be prone to nightmares, and some little girls suddenly develop new fears about dogs, bugs, etc.

Occasionally there may be trouble. A father, emotionally estranged from his wife, may lavish his girl child with the kind of attentions and presents he may have had in mind for her mother. These seductive demonstrations of affection may make it quite difficult for the child to face the reality of her position. She may cling to the fantasy of being Daddy's wife for a precariously long time, with the possibility of its interfering with her later love life. Should her father, on the other hand, be cool and rejecting (or treat her as the boy he longed for), she may run into problems in relating to boys and men as she grows up. There are those who learn to hate men, resent, and fear them—fear being rejected or hurt by them. But these examples are extremes, and are not at all common.

In her classic book *The Second Sex*, Simone de Beauvoir wrote of the girl's need to have a loving father:

> If her father shows affection for his daughter, she feels that her existence is magnificently justified; she is endowed with all the merits that others have to acquire with difficulty; she is fulfilled and deified . . . If her father's love is withheld she may look elsewhere for a valuation of herself and become indifferent to her father or even hostile.

Healthy Sex Attitudes, Identity and Development
Other Suggestions for Helping the Child

It has been suggested by many child psychiatrists that the fewer opportunities the little boy and girl (in our culture) have to see their parents naked during this period, the better. This does not mean that an occasional glimpse of a naked parent is likely to prove traumatic to a very young child. A parent who wants privacy, however, can indicate this without making a fuss. Some parents believe that appearing in the nude will give the child a healthy and wholesome attitude toward the human body. But things do not always work out this way. There is something quite different about feelings engendered by the sight of any human body, statue, or picture, and the sight of one's parents' bodies, especially at this phase of life. The very young child can be sexually excited by seeing his parents' genitals (even wanting to touch and explore them) at a time when this excitement can go nowhere. It also makes good sense to lock bedroom doors during sexual intercourse.

As for having the child, or even a baby over six months, share the parental bedroom, strange as it may seem, noises from the parents' bed as well as their movements can leave obscure but disturbing and indelible impressions on a very young child. He is not always as sound asleep as we would care to believe. In the dark or half-dark, he may be confused and stimulated by what he hears or sees (or imagines he sees). The sounds and motions of his parents' lovemaking, as he gets to be a little older, may be woven into his fantasies and appear to be those of anger and attack instead of love and passion. Even though the child senses somehow that his parents share some special kind of physical intimacy, he is not yet prepared to deal with the overwhelming feelings, the sexual arousal as well as the jealousy and guilt, that can seize him now. This, of course, poses a real problem for parents who live in cramped quarters, and unfortunately, some modern apartments have walls that seem to be made of cardboard. But there are always means of working out this problem—as with most practical problems.

While all of these under-surface trials and conflicts are going

The Roots of Love

on within Johnny and Mary, many wonderful things are taking place on the "outside" too. The child of three or so is now learning how to handle his body more adeptly, his "conversations" are now real conversations, and even his childish opinions often make a lot of sense. (A German saying has it that only little children and fools tell the truth!) He is learning how to work out some of the problems of his daily life, especially the not-always-easy task of sharing with his brother or sister, including the sharing of Mother's and Father's love.

He has colds and runny noses, chicken pox, and the like; he is cranky, moody, sunny, funny, has undecipherable fears and terrors; he becomes babyish again at the oddest moments; he dawdles and drives you crazy; he says cute things and you could eat him up. He now is beginning to dress himself fairly well, and he proudly presents you with his latest work of "art." The world outside of home is not so fearful or bewildering any more, and he is becoming quite fond of some special grownups and little people he has recently met.

Whatever we can do to make his world at home and away from home a full and interesting one, whatever we can do to help him continue to know he has our trust and love and understanding, also will help the inner goings-on move toward their adequate solutions.

By now the child's sexual attitudes, his sex identity and development, along with his capacity to give and receive love, will have taken firm root.

EPILOGUE

 CHAPTER TEN

Where Do We Go from Here?

And they lived happily ever after? Hardly! Growing up, just as life itself, has its pains, disappointments, conflicts, and moments of despair. The child constantly runs into obstacles and hurdles as he moves from one stage of development to another. He runs into new tasks and problems; into physical as well as psychic bumps, into untoward pressures from the outside world, rough words from schoolmates, teachers, and others. And he cannot always maintain that inner sense of well-being and happiness that we have tried so hard to build up in him. According to Anna Freud, "Even the most normal child may feel deeply unhappy for one reason or another, for long or short periods almost every day of his life."

If this is so, then what is it all about? What will we have accomplished up to now and what can we hope for our child's future?

Whatever we have been able to do to foster our child's well-being during these very earliest years will have given him a tremendous head start in life, a growing ability to deal with its difficulties and pains. But more than merely teaching him how to survive, this loving care will teach him how to *live*. Through this special care he will have learned and will continue to learn the joy of touching, tasting, exploring—of savoring life in all its richness, of being able to express himself, and later on to find fulfillment. It will enable him to enjoy the rewards of hard work,

The Roots of Love

to take on commitment and responsibility, and to protect and cherish his loved ones.

A tall order? Yes. Yet the basic philosophy underlying some of the more practical suggestions offered in this book can be adapted and applied to all the future years of child rearing, and beyond. You do what you've done all along, but only more so and in different ways! By now, through "raised-consciousness" about your child, you may begin to respond more sensitively to him, finding your own lives, and enjoyment of your young, deepened and strengthened.

The principles expressed in this book emphasize the helpless infant's basic needs for consistent, tender, and loving care. They continue to stress the young child's need for encouragement and guidance so that he can come to believe in his intrinsic worth and dignity. Through this encouragement he will be able to work not only for recognition—his natural desire to amount to something, to "be *somebody*"—but for his enjoyment of the work itself. And more than this, he will be able to give and accept love—all part of the human condition.

A sense of self-affirmation, self-respect, and self-esteem is the most valuable gift a parent can ever give to his child. From this good self-feeling springs all his qualities of lovingness, of humanity, of the enjoyment of harmonious relationships in his career or job, enabling him to respect those he works with, under, or over, accepting differences, not being shattered by disagreement. Lawrence K. Frank, L.L.D., one of the early leaders of the mental-health movement in this country, once wrote, "Until an individual can live in peace with himself and his private world, he cannot live in peace with his group life."

A child tends to follow what has been called the "self-fulfilling prophecy," which means, broadly, that our young usually behave as we expect (or fear) they will behave. If, as we teach our child what to do and what not to do, we always fear the worst and cloak our attitudes in disapproval—telling him often enough how rotten he is—our attitudes are likely to be reflected in the child's own behavior and self-image. The "Aren't you *ashamed* of yourself!" type of remark cuts deep, even in the earliest years of

Where Do We Go from Here?

life, and the young child, filled with shame and guilt, comes to believe he is worthless and "bad" and acts accordingly. He fears failure besides, convinced he can't make the grade. The reverse is also true—when we expect them to behave decently and have faith in them, children are more apt to live up to these positive expectations. Unburdened by the weight of disapproval and expected failure, they learn to face each new experience in life with the good feelings and positive outlook generated by their previous experiences. "Nothing succeeds like success," as the old adage goes.

But the nagging, negative parental attitudes we often see can be stifling and stunting. It is hard for a young child to shake off anxiety about his own competence and ability to function well. (Without any help from us, he worries about this quite enough.) These attitudes can block off his capacity to grow intellectually and emotionally, and to realize his full potential. Dr. Rollo May, psychotherapist and well-known author and lecturer, recently indicated that when a child's "self-affirmation is blocked, it becomes a compulsive need which drives a person all his life." Dr. May adds another bit of tried and true wisdom, as he writes in his book, *Power and Innocence*:

> Or the child's affirmation of himself may be made difficult in the face of his parents' patterns of, "We love you *only* if you obey us." The child thus gets caught in the destructive aspects of competitiveness, the buying and selling of himself and the world; his self-affirmation is taken by others to be a diminishing of them, and he is diminished in turn by theirs.

All of us work at peak level and give our very most to our efforts when our teachers, employers, or superiors at work encourage us and make us feel we can do a job well. We even can take constructive criticisms favorably when we know they believe in us. And so it goes in our love relationships and friendships. Besides, we move toward those who make us feel good and we pull away from those who denigrate us. Unfortunately for the vulnerable child, he cannot remove himself from denigrating parents.

The Roots of Love

As this book has tried to show, constant battles between parent and child can cause the soil of love to erode, while basically supportive and empathic attitudes replenish this soil. In seeing a child through his difficult, uncertain years of growth ahead, and in helping him to face his problems clearly and realistically, we give him the chance to develop inner resources that will help him to solve or resolve his constantly changing difficulties in future days when he will have to make his way on his own.

Some may protest, "But a child has to be *tough* and *strong* to make it in this difficult world!" Strong is one thing. Tough is another. A tough child or person is usually on the defensive; he is apt to be "weak" or frail in his self-image. He boasts to cover up his fears, he bullies the smaller one to show his "strength," he exploits others—often sexually, not so much to gratify his sexual urges as to use others to make him feel "special" for the moment, or to prove he has power which he knows he lacks.

We need fewer tough people in this world and more quietly strong and loving ones who do not need to declare their strength but who can go about making the world a better one through their compassionate concern for others less fortunate. These are the people whose strength and capacity to love have been cultivated since the days of their infancy. These truly strong ones are those whose warmth reflects the warmth that was given them by their parents or substitutes. The tough and cool ones reflect, in turn, the harshness or coolness of the parents or substitutes who reared *them* in infancy and childhood.

So preoccupied with desperate attempts to overcome their feelings of powerlessness and helplessness, the tough people have little regard for the needs of others. And the self-doubting—the person with a faltering sense of self-love who cannot dare to believe in himself—may also play the game of musical beds. And, if a woman, she may let herself be exploited sexually in order to grasp one brief moment when she feels needed, effective, and important; or she may acquiesce just to please, since she believes that to refuse sexual demands made upon her will cause her to be further unloved or criticized.

We are constantly being warned that the family is "fractured,"

Where Do We Go from Here?

outmoded, useless for today's world, and disappearing. Yet it is within the intimacy of the family—within its protecting walls—that the child's feelings of love are born and cultivated, where he learns to become a civilized and humanized member of his society. Shared experiences, happy and unhappy, within this family—even a loving one-parent family—are etched deeply into a child's memories and become the basis of his later wish to enjoy shared experiences again with his own, new family. No other institution, be it day care, school, commune, etc., can fully substitute for the personal, individualized continuum of loving experiences given to a child by a caring mother and father and other close relatives.

Times and mores have altered continuously since the beginning of man, but throughout history human needs, desires, fears, and conflicts have remained much the same. Among these needs is the wish to cherish and to be cherished, to feel secure in the love of one's mate, and to share exclusivity with that loved one.

Despite all the blasts, all the unfavorable publicity that is given to marriage and the family these days, the institution is still going strong. Witness the stubborn insistence of those who have been divorced to have another crack at it, and the resultant, often more successful remarriages. Witness fathers-to-be joining their wives in prenatal classes, mothers and fathers together at the zoo, eagerly introducing their children to the animal world, or excitedly participating in their children's delight at the circus, or waiting in a long line outside a movie theater—even in the cold or rain—so their child can see a special children's performance. Or look at the numbers of parents at PTA meetings, anxious to learn more about what is best for their children and how to improve their schools; or look at the proud and beaming, sometimes tearful, faces of parents at graduations.

The family may be struggling against enormous odds—a few of which have been mentioned earlier in this book—but by and large it courageously holds its own. The child born into a warm and accepting family that lovingly guides and cherishes him will take full measure of what he has received from it and use this love in all of his human encounters.

The Roots of Love

Nothing is perfect in this world, neither children nor parents—not even love itself. But we can always strive to improve the status quo. Robert Browning believed "A man's reach should exceed his grasp, or what's a heaven for?" We keep on growing emotionally as we learn to understand our own children—and it's a struggle at times. Yet while our imperfections and theirs may never fully disappear, like a pebble dropped into a pond whose ripples widen and widen, so the strength and warmth of our love will reflect on their lives as well as on the lives of others. This goal is surely worth striving for. It is our children's birthright.

Bibliography

ABELIN, ERNEST L. "The Role of the Father in the Separation-Individuation Process." *Separation-Individuation, Essays in Honor of Margaret Mahler.* Edited by John B. McDevitt and Calvin F. Settlage. New York: International Universities Press, 1971.

AINSWORTH, MARY D. SALTER. "The Development of Infant-Mother Attachment." *Review of Child Development Research.* Vol.3. Edited by Bettye M. Caldwell and Henry N. Ricciuti. Chicago: University of Chicago Press, 1973.

———. "Further Research Into the Effects of Maternal Deprivation." *Child Care and the Growth of Love.* By John Bowlby. London: Penguin Books, 1965 (1953).

———. "Object Relations, Dependency and Attachment: A Theoretical Review of the Infant-Mother Relationship." *Child Development,* Vol. 40, 1969.

———, AND BELL, SILVIA M. "Attachment, Exploration and Separation: Illustrated by the Behavior of One-Year-Olds in a Strange Situation." *Child Development,* Vol. 41, 1970 (a).

ANTHONY, E. JAMES. "Folie a Deux: A Developmental Failure in the Process of Separation-Individuation." *Separation-Individuation, Essays in Honor of Margaret S. Mahler.* Edited by John B. McDevitt and Calvin F. Settlage. New York: International Universities Press, 1971.

ARNSTEIN, HELENE S. "The Crisis of Becoming a Father." *Sexual Behavior,* April 1972.

———. "How Babies Learn to Wait." *Parents' Magazine,* December 1970.

———. "That Old-Time Rock." *The New York Times Magazine,* February 4, 1968.

———. *Your Growing Child and Sex.* Indianapolis: Bobbs-Merrill Co., 1967. (Paperback, Avon.)

AUERBACH, ALINE B. *The Why and How of Discipline*. Rev. ed. New York: Child Study Press, 1974.

———. See Wolf, Katherine M.

———. "Can an Infant Be Spoiled?" *Child Study Magazine*, Winter, 1957–8.

BALINT, ALICE. "Love for the Mother and Mother Love." *Primary Love and Psychoanalytic Technique*. Michael Balint. New York: Liveright Publications Corp., 1953.

———. *The Early Years of Life*. New York: Basic Books, 1954.

BALINT, MICHAEL. *Primary Love and Psychoanalytic Technique*. New York: Liveright Publications Corp., 1953.

———. (a) "Primary Love," (b) "Adult Love." *The Basic Fault: Therapeutic Aspects of Regression*. London: Tavistock Publications, 1968. (Distributed in the U.S.A. by Barnes and Noble.)

BEAUVOIR, SIMONE DE. *The Second Sex*. New York: Alfred A. Knopf, 1953. (Paperback, Bantam.)

BELL, SILVIA M., AND AINSWORTH, MARY D. SALTER. "Infant Crying and Maternal Responsiveness." *Child Development*, Vol. 4, 1970 (a).

BENEDEK, THERESE. "Parenthood as a Developmental Phase." *Journal of the American Psychoanalytic Association*, Vol. 7, No. 3, 1959.

———. "The Family as a Psychologic Field"; "The Psychobiology of Pregnancy"; "Motherhood and Nurturing"; and "Fatherhood and Providing." *Parenthood: Its Psychology and Psychopathology*. Edited by E. James Anthony and Therese Benedek. Boston: Little, Brown and Co., 1970.

BENJAMIN, JOHN D. "Further Comments on Some Developmental Aspects of Anxiety." *Counterpoint: Libidinal Object and Subject*. Edited by Herbert S. Gaskill. New York: International Universities Press, 1968.

BERENBERG, SAMUEL. Personal communication.

BETTELHEIM, BRUNO. "How Do You Help Your Children Accept the Harsh Reality of a Divorce and Its Aftermath?" Dialogues With Mothers, *Ladies' Home Journal*, February 1973.

———. "Where Self Begins." *The New York Times Magazine*, February 12, 1967.

BILLER, HENRY B. "Fathering and Female Sexual Development." *Medical Aspects of Human Sexuality*, November 1971.

BLANCK, RUBIN, AND BLANCK, GERTRUDE. *Marriage and Personal Development*. New York: Columbia University Press, 1968.

Bibliography

BOWLBY, JOHN. *Attachment and Loss: Vol. 1. Attachment.* New York: Basic Books, 1969.

———. *Attachment and Loss: Vol. 2. Separation: Anxiety and Anger.* New York: Basic Books, 1973.

———. *Child Care and the Growth of Love.* 2d. ed. London: Penguin Books, 1965 (1953). (In U.S.A., Maryland: Penguin Books.)

———. "Grief and Mourning in Early Childhood." *The Psychoanalytic Study of the Child,* Vol. XV, 1960.

BRAZELTON, T. BERRY. "A Child-Orientated Approach to Toilet Training." *Pediatrics,* Vol. 29 (1), 1962.

———. *Infants and Mothers: Differences in Development.* New York: Delacorte/Seymour Lawrence, 1969. (Paperback, Dell.)

BRENNER, ERMA. *A New Baby! A New Life!* New York: McGraw-Hill Book Co., 1973.

BRODY, SYLVIA. "A Mother Is Being Beaten." *Parenthood: Its Psychology and Psychopathology.* Edited by E. James Anthony and Therese Benedek. Boston: Little, Brown and Co., 1970.

———. "Some Infantile Sources of Childhood Disturbance." *Journal of the American Academy of Child Psychiatry,* Vol. 6, No. 4, 1967.

———. *Patterns of Mothering.* New York: International Universities Press, 1956.

———, AND AXELRAD, SIDNEY. *Anxiety and Ego Formation in Infancy.* New York: International Universities Press, 1970.

BURGNER, MARION, AND EDGECUMBE, ROSE. "Some Problems of the Conceptualization of Early Object Relationships." Part II: "The Concept of Object Constancy." *The Psychoanalytic Study of the Child,* Vol. 27, 1972.

BURLINGHAM, DOROTHY. "The Pre-Oedipal Infant-Father Relationship." *The Psychoanalytic Study of the Child,* Vol. 28, 1973.

———. See Freud, Anna.

CALDWELL, BETTYE M. "Infant Day Care and Attachment." *American Journal of Orthopsychiatry,* Vol. 4, No. 3, 1970.

———. "The Effects of Infant Care." *Review of Child Development Research.* Vol. 1. Edited by Martin L. Hoffman and Lois Wladis Hoffman. New York: Russell Sage Foundation, 1964.

———. "What Does Research Tell Us About Day Care?: For Children Under Three." *Children Today,* Vol. 1, No. 1, 1972.

CHASIN, MARIE H., AND CHASIN, RICHARD. "Parents Have Pasts."

Pregnancy, Birth and the Newborn Baby: A Publication for Parents. The Boston Children's Medical Center, New York: Delacorte/Seymour Lawrence, 1972.

CLOWER, VIRGINIA L. Panel Report: "The Development of the Child's Sense of His Sexual Identity." *Journal of the American Psychoanalytic Association,* Vol. 18, No. 1, 1970.

COLMAN, ARTHUR D., AND COLMAN, LIBBY L. *Pregnancy: The Psychological Experience.* New York: Herder and Herder, 1971.

DESPERT, J. LOUIS. *Children of Divorce.* Rev. ed. New York: Doubleday & Co. 1963. (Paperback, also.)

EDGECUMBE, ROSE, AND BURGNER, MARION. "Some Problems in the Conceptualization of Early Object Relationships. Part 1. The Concepts of Need Satisfaction and Need Satisfying Relationships." *The Psychoanalytic Study of the Child,* Vol. 27, 1972.

EHRHARDT, A. A.; EPSTEIN, R.; AND MONEY, J. "Foetal Androgens and Female Gender Identity in the Early Treated Andrenogenital Syndrome." *Johns Hopkins Medical Journal,* Vol. 122, 1968.

EHRLICH, SHIRLEY STENDIG. "The Psychological Impact of New Parenthood." *Pregnancy, Birth and the Newborn Baby: A Publication for Parents.* The Boston Children's Medical Center, New York: Delacorte/Seymour Lawrence, 1972.

ERIKSON, ERIK H. *Childhood and Society.* Rev. ed. New York: W. W. Norton & Co., 1964 (1950).

———. "Identity and the Life Cycle: Selected Papers." *Psychological Issues,* Monograph 1, Vol. 1, No. 1, 1959.

ESCALONA, SIBYLLE. "Emotional Development in the First Year of Life." *Problems of Infancy and Childhood.* Edited by Milton Senn. New York: Josiah Macy Jr. Foundation, 1953.

———. *Understanding Hostility in Children.* Chicago: Science Research Associates, 1970.

FAIRBAIRN, W. RONALD D. "Object Relations Theory of the Personality." *Psychoanalytic Studies of the Personality.* London: Tavistock Publications, 1952.

FARBER, SUSAN L., ed. "Issues in Early Day Care." Papers by Sibylle K. Escalona, Roy K. Lilleskov, Werner Muensterberger, Peter B. Neubauer, Eleanor Pavenstedt, Sally Provence, and Albert J. Solnit. *Psychosocial Process,* Vol. 3, No. 1, 1974.

FLEMING, JOAN. "Early Object Deprivation and Transference Phenomena." *Psychoanalytic Quarterly,* Vol. XLI, No. 1, 1972.

Bibliography

FRAIBERG, SELMA H. "How A Baby Learns to Love." *Redbook Magazine*, May 1971.

———. "Libidinal Object Constancy and Mental Representation." *The Psychoanalytic Study of the Child*, Vol. XXIV, 1969.

———. *The Magic Years: Understanding and Handling the Problems of Early Childhood*. New York: Charles Scribner's & Sons, 1959. (Paperback, Lyceum.)

———. "The Origins of Human Bonds." *Commentary*, December 1967.

FRANK, LAWRENCE K. *Society as the Patient: Essays on Culture and Personality*. New Brunswick: Rutgers University Press, 1949.

FREUD, ANNA. *The Ego and the Mechanisms of Defense. The Writings of Anna Freud* (1936). Vol. 2. New York: International Universities Press, 1973.

———. *Indications for Child Analysis and Other Papers. The Writings of Anna Freud* (1945–56). Vol. 4. New York: International Universities Press, 1968.

———. *Normality and Pathology in Childhood*. New York: International Universities Press, 1965.

———, in collaboration with Dorothy Burlingham, *Infants Without Families* (1939–45). New York: International Universities Press, 1944.

FREUD, SIGMUND. "Beyond the Pleasure Principle" (1920). Vol. 28. *Standard Edition*. London: Hogarth Press, 1955.

———. "Civilization and Its Discontents" (1930). Vol. 21. *Standard Edition*. London: Hogarth Press, 1961.

———. "On Narcissism: An Introduction" (1914). Vol. 14. *Standard Edition*. London: Hogarth Press, 1957.

———. "On the Sexual Theories of Children" (1908). Vol. 9. *Standard Edition*. London: Hogarth Press, 1959.

———. "Three Essays on the Theory of Sexuality" (1905). Vol. 7. *Standard Edition*. London: Hogarth Press, 1953.

———. *The Complete Introductory Lectures on Psycho-Analysis* (1915–33). New York: W. W. Norton & Co., 1966.

FRIEDMAN, LAWRENCE J. "Ambivalence and the Vicissitudes of the Oedipal Complex." *The Israel Annals of Psychiatry and Related Disciplines*, Vol. 3, October 1965.

FROMM, ERICH. *The Art of Loving*. New York: Harper & Brothers, 1956.

FURST, SIDNEY S., ed. *Psychic Trauma*. New York: Basic Books, 1967.

GELEERD, ELISABETH R. "The Beginnings of Aggressiveness in Children." *Child Study Magazine*, Vol. 34, No. 4, Fall 1957.

GILBERT, SARA D. *Three Years to Grow: Guidance for Your Child's First Three Years.* New York: Parents' Magazine Press, 1972.

GOLDBERG, SUSAN, AND LEWIS, MICHAEL. "Play Behavior in the Year-Old Infant: Early Sex Differences." *Child Development,* Vol. 40, 1969.

GREENACRE, PHYLLIS. "Childhood of the Artist: Libidinal Phase, Development and Giftedness," *Emotional Growth,* Vol. 2. New York: International Universities Press, 1971.

———. "Considerations Regarding the Parent-Infant Relationship." *International Journal of Psycho-Analysis,* Vol. XII, 1960.

———. "Early Physical Determinants in the Development of a Sense of Identity." *Journal of the American Psychoanalytic Association,* Vol. 6, No. 4, 1958.

———. "The Primal Scene and the Sense of Reality." *Psychoanalytic Quarterly,* Vol. XLII, No. 1, 1973.

———. *Trauma, Growth and Personality.* New York: International Universities Press, 1970 (1952).

GREENSON, RALPH. "Dis-identifying From Mother: Its Special Importance for the Boy." *International Journal of Psycho-Analysis,* Vol. 49, 1968.

HANDLESMAN, IRVING. "The Effects of Early Object Relationships on Sexual Development." *The Psychoanalytic Study of the Child,* Vol. XX, 1965.

HARLOW, HARRY F. "Love in Infant Monkeys." *Scientific American,* June 1959.

———. "The Development of Affectional Patterns in Infant Monkeys." *Determinants of Infant Behavior,* Vol. 1. Edited by B. M. Foss. New York: John Wiley & Sons, 1958.

———, AND HARLOW, MARGARET H. "A Study of Animal Affection." *Natural History,* December 1961.

HARTLEY, RUTH E. "Children's Concepts of Male and Female Roles." *Merrill-Palmer Quarterly,* Vol. 6, 1960.

HEINICKE, CHRISTOPH M., AND WESTHEIMER, ILSE. *Brief Separations.* New York: International Universities Press, 1965.

HOFFER, WILLIE. "Mouth, Hand and Ego Integration." *The Psychoanalytic Study of the Child,* Vol. III/IV, 1949.

HOLT, LUTHER EMMETT. *The Care and Feeding of Infants and Children.* (1894) 14th revised edition by L. Emmett Holt, Jr., 1929. New York and London: D. Appleton Co.

Bibliography

HOOVER, MARY B. *The Responsive Parent: Meeting the Realities of Parenthood Today.* New York: Parents' Magazine Press, 1972.

———. "How Children Test a Marriage," *Parents' Magazine*, April 1970.

JACOBSON, EDITH. "The Development of the Wish for a Child in Boys." *The Psychoanalytic Study of the Child*, Vol. V, 1950.

———. *The Self and the Object World.* New York: International Universities Press, 1964.

JESSNER, LUCIE; WEIGERT, EDITH; AND FOY, JAMES L. "The Development of Parental Attitudes During Pregnancy." *Parenthood: Its Psychology and Psychopathology.* Edited by E. James Anthony and Therese Benedek. Boston: Little, Brown and Co., 1970.

KAGAN, JEROME. See Lang, Cynthia.

KAUFMAN, BEL. "A Mother's Love." *Today's Health*, May 1972.

KESTENBERG, JUDITH. "Vicissitudes of Female Sexuality." *Journal of the American Psychoanalytic Association*, Vol. 4, No. 2, 1956.

KIERKEGAARD, SÖREN. *Purity of Heart* (1846) New York: Harper & Brothers, 1938.

KLEEMAN, JAMES A. "A Boy Discovers His Penis." *The Psychoanalytic Study of the Child*, Vol. XX, 1965.

———. "Hatching Out." *The New York Times Magazine*, February 9, 1969.

———. "The Establishing of Core Gender Identity in Normal Girls." I. (a) "Introduction"; (b) "Development of the Ego Capacity to Differentiate." II. "How Meanings Are Conveyed Between Parent and Child in the First Three Years." *Archives of Sexual Behavior*, Vol. 1, No. 2, 1971.

———. "The Peek-A-Boo Game." Part 1. "Its Origins, Meanings and Related Phenomena in the First Year." *The Psychoanalytic Study of the Child*, Vol. XXII. 1967.

LANG, CYNTHIA. "The Real Difference Between the Sexes: An Interview with Jerome Kagan." *Parents' Magazine*, September 1973.

LEEUWEN, KATO VAN, AND POMER, SIDNEY L. "The Separation-Adaptation to Temporary Object Loss." *Journal of the American Academy of Child Psychology*, Vol. 8, No. 4, 1969.

LESHAN, EDA. *Natural Parenthood: Raising Your Child Without a Script.* New York: New American Library, 1970.

LIDZ, THEODORE. "The Effects of Children on Marriage." *The Marriage*

Relationship. Edited by Salo Rosenbaum and Ian Alger. New York: Basic Books, 1968.

———. *The Person: His Development Throughout the Life Cycle.* New York: Basic Books, 1968.

LILEY, H. M. I., AND DAY, BETH. *Modern Motherhood: Pregnancy, Childbirth and the Newborn Baby.* Revised edition. New York: Random House, 1969.

MACCOBY, ELEANOR E., AND FELDMAN, S. SHIRLEY. "Mother-Attachment and Stranger Reactions in the Third Year of Life." *Monographs of the Society for Research in Child Development,* Serial No. 146, Vol. 37, No. I, March 1972.

———, ed. *The Development of Sex Differences.* Stanford: Stanford University Press, 1966.

MAHLER, MARGARET S., "Rapprochement Subphase of the Separation-Individuation Process." *Psychoanalytic Quarterly,* Vol. XLI, No. 4, 1972.

———. In collaboration with Furer, Manuel. *On Human Symbiosis and the Vicissitudes of Individuation.* Vol. 1, *Infantile Psychosis.* New York: International Universities Press, 1968.

———, AND McDEVITT, JOHN B. "Observations on Adaptation and Defense in Statu Nascendi: Developmental Precursors in the First Two Years of Life." *Psychoanalytic Quarterly,* Vol. XXXVII, No. 1, 1968.

———, and LA PERRIERE, KITTY. "Mother-Child Interaction During Separation-Individuation." *Psychoanalytic Quarterly,* Vol. 34, No. 4, 1965.

MAY, ROLLO. *Power and Innocence: A Search for the Sources of Violence.* New York: W. W. Norton & Co., 1972.

MAYER, GRETA, AND HOOVER, MARY. *Learning to Love and Let Go: A Guide to Helping Children Become Independent.* A Child Study Association Publication, 1965.

McDERMOTT, JOHN F., JR. "Parental Divorce in Early Childhood." *American Journal of Psychiatry,* Vol. 124, No. 10, 1968.

MEAD, MARGARET. *Blackberry Winter: My Earlier Years.* New York: William Morrow & Company, 1972. (Paperback, A Touchstone Book—Simon and Schuster.)

———. *Sex and Temperament in Three Primitive Societies.* New York: William Morrow & Co., 1935. (Paperback, Mentor Books, New American Library.)

Bibliography

———. "Childbirth in a Changing World." *Pregnancy, Birth and the Newborn Baby: A Publication for Parents.* The Boston Children's Medical Center. New York: Delacorte/Seymour Lawrence, 1972.

MENNINGER, KARL., with the collaboration of Menninger, Jeanette Lyle. *Love Against Hate.* New York: Harcourt, Brace & Co., 1942.

MEYER, RUBEN; LEVITT, MORTON; FALICK, MORDECAI L.: AND RUBENSTEIN, BEN O. *Essentials of Pediatric Psychiatry.* New York: Appleton-Century-Crofts, 1962.

MODELL, ARNOLD H. *Object Love and Reality.* New York: International Universities Press, 1968.

MONEY, JOHN. "Determinants of Human Sexual Identity and Behavior." *Progress in Group and Family Therapy.* Edited by Clifford J. Sager and Helen Singer Kaplan. New York: Brunner/Mazel Publishers, 1972.

———. "An Examination of Some Basic Sexual Concepts: the Evidence of Human Hermaphroditism." *Bulletin, Johns Hopkins Hospital*, Vol. 97, 1955.

———, AND EHRHARDT, ANKE A. *Man, Woman, Boy, Girl—Differentiation and Dimorphism of Gender Identity from Conception to Maturity.* Baltimore: Johns Hopkins University Press, 1972.

MORRIS, DESMOND. *Intimate Behavior.* New York: Random House, 1971.

MURPHY, LOIS BARCLAY. "Preventive Implications of Mental Disorders in the Preschool Years." *Prevention of Mental Disorders in Children.* Edited by Gerald Caplan. New York: Basic Books, 1961.

———, and associates. *The Widening World of Childhood: Paths Towards Mastery.* New York: Basic Books, 1962.

NEUBAUER, PETER B. "The One-Parent Child and His Oedipal Development." The *Psychoanalytic Study of the Child*, Vol. 15, 1960.

———. Personal communication.

NICHOLS, EDWIN. Personal communication.

OLDEN, CHRISTINE. "Notes on the Development of Empathy." *The Psychoanalytic Study of the Child*, Vol. XIII, 1953.

PARENS, HENRI, AND SAUL, LEON J. *Dependence in Man: A Psychoanalytic Study.* New York: International Universities Press, 1971.

PIAGET, JEAN. *The Construction of Reality in the Child.* New York: Basic Books, 1954.

PINE, FRED. "On the Separation Process: Universal Trends and Individual Differences. *Separation-Individuation: Essays in Honor of*

The Roots of Love Margaret Mahler. Edited by John B. McDevitt and Calvin F. Settlage. New York: International Universities Press, 1971.

POGREBIN, LETTY COTTIN. "Motherhood." *Ms., May 1973.*

PULVER, SIDNEY E. "Narcissism: The Term and the Concept." *Journal of the American Psychoanalytic Association*, Vol. 18, No. 2, 1970.

REICH, ANNIE. "Narcissistic Object Choice in Women." *Journal of the American Psychoanalytic Association*, Vol. 1, No. 1, 1953.

ROBERTSON, JAMES AND JOYCE. "Young Children in Brief Separation: A Fresh Look." *The Psychoanalytic Study of the Child*, Vol. 36, 1971.

ROBSON, KENNETH S. "The Role of Eye-to-Eye Contact in Maternal Infant Attachment." *Journal of Child Psychiatry*, Vol. 8, 1967.

ROCHLIN, GREGORY. *Grief and Discontents.* Boston: Little, Brown and Co., 1965.

ROIPHE, ANNE RICHARDSON. *Up the Sandbox.* New York: Simon and Schuster. (Paperback, Fawcett, Crest.)

———. "Family War: Can You Win?" *Vogue*, June 1973.

ROIPHE, HERMAN. "On An Early Genital Phase." *The Psychoanalytic Study of the Child*, Vol. XXIII, 1968.

ROSS, JAMES B., AND MCLAUGHLIN, MARY M. *A Portable Medieval Reader.* New York: Viking Press, 1949.

RUBINFINE, DAVID L. "Maternal Stimulation, Psychic Structure, and Early Object Relations: With Special Reference to Aggression and Denial." *The Psychoanalytic Study of the Child*, Vol. XVII, 1962.

SALK, LEE, AND KRAMER, RITA. *How to Raise a Human Being.* New York: Random House, 1969. (Paperback, Paperback Library.)

SCHAFFER, H. R., AND EMERSON, PEGGY. "Patterns of Response to Physical Contact in Early Human Development." *Journal of Child Psychology and Psychiatry*, Vol. 5, No. 1, 1964.

———. "The Development of Social Attachments in Infancy." *Monographs of the Society for Research in Child Development*, Vol. 29, No. 3, 1964.

SCHECTER, DAVID E. "Of Human Bonds and Bondage." *In the Name of Life: Essays in Honor of Erich Fromm.* New York: Holt, Rinehart and Winston, 1971.

———. "On the Emergence of Human Relatedness." *Interpersonal Explorations in Psychoanalysis.* Edited by Earl Wittenberg. New York: Basic Books, 1973.

Bibliography

———. "Infant Development." *American Handbook of Psychiatry.* Rev. 2nd. ed. Edited by Silvano Arieti. New York: Basic Books, 1974.

SHAYWITZ, SALLY E. "Catch 22 For Mothers: Is Mommy Necessary?" *The New York Times Magazine*, March 4, 1973.

SHEVRIN, HOWARD AND TOUSSIENG, POVL W. "Vicissitudes of the Need for Tactile Stimulation in Instinctual Development." *The Psychoanalytic Study of the Child*, Vol. XX, 1965.

SOLKOFF, NORMAN; YAFFE, SUMNER; WEINTRAUB, DAVID; AND BLASE, BARBARA. "Effects of Handling on the Subsequent Development of Premature Infants." *Developmental Psychology*, Vol. 1, No. 6, 1969.

SOLNIT, ALBERT J. "Aggression: A View of Theory Building in Psychoanalysis." *Journal of the American Psychoanalytic Association*, Vol. XX, No. 3, 1972.

———. "A Study of Object Loss in Infancy." *The Psychoanalytic Study of the Child*, Vol. XXV, 1970.

———. "Some Adaptive Functions of Aggressive Behavior." *Psychoanalysis: A General Psychology*. Edited by Rudolph M. Loewenstein, Lottie M. Newman, Max Schur, and Albert J. Solnit. New York: International Universities Press, 1966.

SPITZ, RENÉ A. "Aggression: Its Role in the Establishment of Object Relations." *Drives, Affects, Behavior*, Vol. 1. Edited by Rudolph M. Loewenstein. New York: International Universities Press, 1953.

———. "Autoeroticism Re-Examined." *The Psychoanalytic Study of the Child*, Vol. XVII, 1962.

———. "Life and the Dialogue." *Counterpoint: Libidinal Object and Subject.* Edited by Herbert S. Gaskill. New York: International Universities Press, 1963.

———. "Metapsychology and Infant Observation." *Psychoanalysis—A General Psychology.* Edited by Rudolph M. Loewenstein, Lottie M. Newman, Max Schur, and Albert J. Solnit. New York: International Universities Press, 1966.

———. *The First Year of Life.* New York: International Universities Press, 1965.

SPOCK, BENJAMIN, AND REINHART, JOHN. *A Baby's First Year.* New York: Pocket Books, 1964 (1955).

———. *Dr. Spock Talks With Mothers.* New York: Paperback-Crest Book. Fawcett World Library, 1964 (1961).

———. *Raising Children in a Difficult World.* New York: W. W. Norton & Co. 1974.

Index

adventurous tendencies, 101–5
aggression, 4–8
Ainsworth, Dr. Mary D. Salter, 53
anger, 4–5
anger control, 131–9; and fear of loss of love, 132–7; and parental discipline, 139–43; parental handling, 137–9; and parents' manipulation, 136–7
Anthony, Dr. E. James, 104n
Arapesh tribe, 14–15
attention-seeking, 115–17
attitude development, and feeding, 48–50
Auerbach, Aline B., 119, 143
Axelrad, Dr. Sidney, 49, 50, 73

babies. *See* infant
"baby blues," 31–2
de Beauvoir, Simone, 198
Bell, Dr. Silvia M., 53
Benedek, Dr. Therese, 28–9, 110
Berenberg, Dr. Samuel, 60, 61
Bettelheim, Dr. Bruno, 168
birth fantasies, 184–6
birth, reactions to by elder child, 143–50; empathizing with

birth— (cont.)
child, 144–5, 146–8; explanation of to child, 146; later reactions to sibling, 148–50; preparing elder child for, 145–6
bladder and bowel control, 125–31; early vs. later training, 126–31; motivation for, 129–31
bottle- vs. breast-feeding, 46–7
bottle, weaning from, 94–5
bowel and bladder control, 125–31; early vs. later training, 126–31; motivation for, 129–31
Bowlby, Dr. John, 9, 102
breast- vs. bottle-feeding, 46–7
breast, weaning from, 92–4
Brody, Dr. Sylvia, 49, 50, 73, 74, 140
Browning, Robert (quoted), 208
Burlingham, Dorothy, 9

Caldwell, Bettye M., 162–3
castration anxiety, 179, 195
children. *See* infant
colicky babies, 54

Colman, Dr. Arthur, 29
Colman, Libby Lee, 29
conscience, development of, 141
couvade, 181
cradling, 59–61
crying, baby's, 51–75; pacifying of, 58–72; significance of, 51–4; soothing of, 59–70

day-care centers, 160–3; and the under-threes, 162–3
disciplining, parental, 139–43
divorce and the child, 168–74; and child's guilts and fears, 172–4; and infant under two, 169–70; and infant two to three, 171–2

Ehrhardt, Dr. Anke A., 187
Erikson, Dr. Erik H., 40, 128
Escalona, Dr. Sybille, 132
exploring tendencies, 101–5

father, emulation of by boy, 196–7
father, girl's need for, 198
fatherliness, characteristics of, 28–9
father's role, 26–31
fears and guilts, childhood, 172–4
feeding, 45–50; and attitude development, 48–50; bottle vs. breast, 46–7; and love relationship, 45–50
Fraiberg, Dr. Selma, 56, 140

Frank, Lawrence K., 204
Frederick II, Emperor of Rome, 8
Freud, Anna, 9, 92, 203
Freud, Dr. Sigmund, 182
Friedman, Dr. Lawrence J., 181, 184
Fromm, Dr. Erich, 41
frustration, 7; learning to tolerate, 73–5

genital self-discovery, 176–8; boys, 176–7; girls, 177–8
Goldberg, Susan, 188
grandparents, 22–6
Greenacre, Dr. Phyllis, 101
Gruenberg, Sidonie Matsner, 180n
guidance, parental, principles of, 203–8
guilts and fears, childhood, 172–4

Harlow, Dr. Harry H., 46
hate, 4–5
Hoffer, Dr. Willie, 4
Holt, Dr. L. Emmett, 59
hormone differences, and sex identity, 187

impulse control, 125–50
indulgence and permissiveness, 112–13
infant, societal influence on, 14–17
infant, spoiling of, 72–5

Index

infant, to six months, love needs of, 37–57; baby's cries, significance of, 51–4; baby's smile, significance of, 54–7; colicky babies, 54; development of reactions, 38–41; and feeding, 45–50; mother/child communication, development of, 43–5; and mother-substitutes, 42–3; newborn infant, 37–8; and trust, 38–41
infant, to six months, pacifying of, 58–72
infant, six to twelve months, and development of love capacity, 79–97; love-reaction to objects, 91–2; mother-substitutes, objects as, 91–2; separation from mother, 83–90, 95–7, 153–74; reactions to strangers, 81–3; weaning, emotional aspects of, 92–5; and working mother, 88–90
infant, one to two years, 101–21; adventurous tendencies, 101–5; attention-seeking, 115–17; and mother/child relationship, 105–7, 109–12; narcissism, 116–17; negative reactions, 107–9, 111; parental reactions to behavior, 109–12; and parental self-esteem, 114; and permissiveness and indulgence, 112–13; separation fears, 117–21; sleeping problems, 117–21
infant, to two years, and divorce, 169–70
infant, two to three years, and divorce, 171–2
infant, two to three years, and impulse control, 125–50; anger control, 131–9; bowel and bladder control, 125–31; jealousy and rivalry, coping with, 143–50; and parental disciplining, 139–43
infant, to three years, and parental guidance, 203–8
infant, to three years, and separations from parents, 83–90, 95–7, 153–74; day-care centers, 160–3; divorce, 168–74; nursery school, 154–60; parental vacations, 163–8
infant, to three years, and sex, 175–200; birth fantasies, 184–6; sex attitudes, 175–84; sex development, 193–200; sexual identity and sex roles, 186–93

Jacobson, Dr. Edith, 134
jealousy and rivalry, coping with, 143–50; birth, explaining to child, 146; empathizing with child, 144–5, 146–8; later reactions to sibling, 148–50; preparing child for birth of sibling, 145–6

Kagan, Dr. Jerome, 189
Kierkegaard, Sören, 104
Kleeman, Dr. James A., 177, 187, 191

Lang, Cynthia, 189
Lewis, Michael, 189
Lidz, Dr. Theodore, 20, 22, 125, 126, 195
love, fear of losing, 132–7
love, power of in early life, 3–17; aggression, positiveness of, 5–8; anger, hate and aggression in infant, 4–5; child development and societal influence, 14–17; early love as a model for later life, 4; love starvation, effects of, 8–10; and parental influence, 10–14
love relationship, and feeding, 45–50
love, used as a parental weapon instead of as a tool, 136–7

McDevitt, Dr. John B., 104n
Mahler, Dr. Margaret S., 95, 96, 101, 102, 138, 153
marital roles, 20
marriage, effects of parenthood on, 19–34
masturbation, 177, 178–9
"maternity blues," 31–2
May, Dr. Rollo, 205
Mead, Dr. Margaret, 14–15, 183
Milne, A. A. (quoted), 153
Money, Dr. John, 187
Morris, Dr. Desmond, 62
mother/child relationship, 105–7, 109–12, *passim;* development of communication, 43–5; first reactions to baby, 32–3; temperamental interaction, 33–4

motherhood, 11–14; new mother's relationship to her own mother, 22–5
mother-substitutes, 42–3, 91–2
motion, soothing, 62–3
Mundugumor tribe, 14, 15–16
Murphy, Dr. Lois B., 50, 66, 156

narcissism, 116–17
Neubauer, Dr. Peter B., 45, 85, 166
Nichols, Edwin, 28
nursery school, 154–60; parental reactions to, 159–60

objects, love-reactions to, 91–2
Oedipus complex, 193–7; and castration anxiety, 179, 195

pacifying, 58–72
parental disciplining, 139–43
parental guidance, principles of, 203–8
parental reactions, 109–12
parental self-esteem, 114
parental vacations, without child, 163–8; need for, 163–5; planning of, 165–6; reactions to return, 166–8
parenthood, effects on marriage, 19–34; and marital roles, 20; and "maternity blues," 31–2; and mother/baby temperamental interaction, 33–4; and mother's first reactions to

Index

parenthood—(cont.)
   baby, 32–3; and new mother's relationship with her mother, 22–5; and role of father, 26–31; and role of grandparents, 25–6

penis envy, 182

permissiveness and indulgence, 112–13

Piaget, Dr. Jean, 84, 145

reactions, development of, 38–41

reactions, parental, 109–12; of mother, 32–3

rivalry and jealousy, coping with, 143–50; birth, explaining to child, 146; empathizing with child, 144–5, 146–8; later reactions to sibling, 148–50; preparing child for birth of sibling, 145–6

rocking chairs, for soothing, 61–2

Roiphe, Anne Richardson, 47, 106

roles, sexual, 186–93; sex role identity, 191–3

Salimbene, 8

Salk, Dr. Lee, 69

Schecter, Dr. David E., 71

self-discovery, genital, 176–8; boys, 176–7; girls, 177–8

self-esteem, parental, 114

separation fears, 117–21

separations, reactions to, 83–90, 95–7, 153–74; brief separations, 85–8; day-care centers, 160–3; divorce, 168–74; nursery school, 154–60; parental vacations, 163–8

Settlage, Dr. Calvin F., 104n

sex attitudes, 175–86; and birth fantasies, 184–6; development of, 175–6; discovery of sex differences, boys, 179–82; discovery of sex differences, girls, 182–4; genital self-discovery, boys, 176–7; genital self-discovery, girls, 177–8; and masturbation, 177, 178–9

sex differences, child's perception of in adults, 191

sex differences, discovery of, 179–84; boys, 179–82; girls, 182–4

sex identity and sex roles, 186–93; and choice of toys, 188–90; and hormonal sex differences, 187; perception of adult sex differences, 191; and sex role identity, 191–93

sexual development, 193–200; boys, 195–7; girls, 197–8; and Oedipus complex, 193–7; parental help in, 199–200

sleeping problems, 117–21

smile, baby's, significance of, 54–7

social influences, 14–17

Solnit, Dr. Albert J., 6, 167

soothing, 59–70; by cradling, 59–61; by motion, 62–3; by rocking chair, 61–2; by sound,

soothing— (cont.)
68–70; by sucking, 66–8; by touch, 63–6
sound, for soothing, 68–70
spanking, 139–43; and development of conscience, 141; long-term results of, 140–1; misconceptions about, 141–3
Spitz, Dr. René, 9, 59
starvation, love, 8–10
Stevenson, Adlai E. (quoted), 26
Stoller, Dr. Robert J., 188
strangers, reactions to, 81–3
sucking, for soothing, 66–8
Sullivan, Dr. Harry Stack, 115

tantrums. *See* anger control
thumb-sucking, 67–8, 110

toilet training, 125–31; early vs. later training, 126–31; motivation for, 129–31
touch, for soothing, 63–6
toy choice, and sexual identity, 188–90
trust, development of, 38–41

vacations, parental, 163–8

weaning, emotional aspects of, 92–5; from bottle, 94–5; from breast, 92–4
Winnicott, Dr. D. W., 43, 72, 91
Wolf, Dr. Katherine B., 119
Wolff, Dr. Peter H., 38, 42, 55
working mothers, 88–90

Young, Leontine, 107–8